The Best Python Programming Step-By-Step Beginners Guide

Easily Master Software engineering with Machine Learning, Data Structures, Syntax, Django Object-Oriented Programming, and AI application

Chris Williamson

Table of Contents

Introduction

Python is widely regarded as the next generation programming language. It was designed by Guido van Rossum at the CWI and has become a widely used high-level and general purpose programming language. There are certain pre-requisites for the language, though, which can be really helpful while learning. If you have any prior knowledge of other programming languages, it will be a huge benefit.

There are many reasons why the programming language is so popular. It places emphasis on readability of codes, ease of writing them, and shorter codes. Python programmers can explain the logical concepts within a few lines of code, unlike other languages such as Java or C++. It supports several programming paradigms such as OOP, functional and imperative programming, or even procedural programming. You can find inbuilt functions for almost every commonly used concept. "Simple is best" is the philosophy used by Python.

Some features:

1. It comes interpreted: You will not find any separate execution and compilation steps such as those on C and C++. You may run the program directly from the source code. Python converts the source code internally into an intermediate form which is called bytecodes. It is then translated into the native language used by the computer for running it. There is no requirement of linking the code to libraries or loading it with them.

2. It is independent of platforms: You can develop the Python programs and execute them on several OS platforms. You may use Python on Windows, Linux, Mac, Solaris, etc.

3. It is redistributable, free, and open source.

4. It is a high-level language: There is no need to take care of low-level details in Python programming like managing the memory of the programs.

5. Simple, Robust, and Embeddable: Python is close to the English language and so is simple to learn. The emphasis is more on the problem solution rather than syntax. It can be used with C or C++ programs for providing scripting capabilities to the program users. It comes with exceptional handling features and in-built memory management techniques.

6. It has rich library support: You will find that the Python standard library is very big. Python uses the philosophy "batteries included" and so it can help with many things such as regular expressions, unit testing, databases, CGI, web browsers, threading, documentation generation, email, HTML, XML, cryptography, WAV files, and GUI. And much more. Apart from providing the standard library support, there are many other high-quality libraries available like the Python Imaging Library. It is an exceptionally easy image manipulation library.

A comparison between Python and Java

Python is dynamically typed while Java is statically typed. In Python, there is no need for declaring anything, while in Java all variable names and their types have to be explicitly declared. There is an assignment statement which binds some name to an object in Python, and this object can be of any type, while in Java attempting to assign some object of the incorrect type to a variable name will trigger an exception.

In Python, there is no typecasting needed while using container objects, whereas in Java type casting is necessary for using container objects. Python is more concise and expresses a lot in limited words, while Verbose consists of more words. Python is also more compact than Java. For structuring the code Python uses indentation, while Java uses braces.

Let's check the classic Hello World program for illustrating relative verbosity of Java programs and Python programs. The Java code for this looks like:

```java
public class HelloWorld

{

   public static void main (String[] args)

   {

      System.out.println("Hello, world!");

   }

}
```

While the Python code would be:

```python
print "Hello, world!"

print("Hello, world!") # Python version 3
```

There are some similarities between the two programming languages, however. They both need some form of runtime on the system called JVM or Python runtime. They can be compiled to executables possibly without any runtime. It is situational and none of them are developed to work in this manner.

There are two versions of Python available at the moment, and they are Python 2 and Python 3. Most beginners will be wondering which of them to use to make a start. The answer to that query is normally something along the lines of, "Just go with your favorite tutorial and check out the variations later."

Software that uses Python

Python is successfully embedded in several software products as a scripting language. The GNU debugger will use Python as a pretty printer for displaying complicated structures like C++ containers. Python is extensively used in AI (Artificial Intelligence). It is often used for tasks related to natural language processing.

Python Current Applications

There are a number of Linux distributors who make use of installers that are written in Python. A common example is Ubuntu's Ubiquity. Python is used extensively in the information security industry and also in exploit development. The single board computer Raspberry makes use of Python as the main user-programming language. The programming language is used in the game development sector as well. The pros of Python include its simplicity and the multi-paradigm approach. The main disadvantage is the slower speed of operation compared to C and C++. It doesn't work with browsers and mobile computing. For C and C++ programmers, going to Python is irritating, as the language needs good code indentation. Some of the variable names that are commonly used in C and C++ such as sum are functions in Python.

Therefore the C and C++ programmers must look out for them.

Industrial Significance

Almost all organizations these days are looking for candidates who know about Python programming. People who have knowledge of Python are more likely to impress the interview panel. Therefore, it is a good idea for beginners to start learning Python and excel in it.

Chapter 1: Python Features, Philosophy & Applications

Python Features

Python is comparable to Java, Ruby, Scheme, or Perl because it is powerful and is a clear OOP language. Some notable features of Python are:

- It has an elegant syntax thereby making the written programs simple to read. Basically, it is easy to use a programming language which makes it stress-free for getting your program to work. It makes Python suitable for prototype development and other ad-hoc programming tasks without any compromise on maintainability.

- Python is available with a huge standard library which supports several common programming tasks like the connection to web servers, looking for text with regular expressions, and reading and modifying files. It has an interactive mode which makes it simple to test short code snippets. You can also find IDLE or a bundled development environment.

- Python can be simply extended by adding newer modules implemented in compiled languages like C or C++. Python can also be embedded into applications for providing a programmable interface.

- Python can run on any OS including Windows, Mac,

Linux, and UNIX, and there are some unofficial builds available for Android and iOS. Python is free software in 2 senses. You are not required to pay anything to download or use Python, or to include it in your applications. It can be easily modified and redistributed, and although the programming language is copyrighted, it is available with an open source license.

The following programming language features are available on Python:

- You can find a range of fundamental data types on Python. Numbers including complex, floating point, and unlimited length long integers; strings including both Unicode and ASCII, dictionaries, and lists. It also supports OOP and its classes having multiple inheritances. Its code may be grouped into packages and modules.

- Python programming languages will catch and raise exceptions resulting in clean error handling. The data types are dynamically and strongly typed. By mixing the incompatible types, for instance, attempting to add a number to a string will cause an exception to be raised, therefore the errors are caught earlier. It also contains advanced programming features like generators and list comprehension.

- The automatic memory management of Python means you are free from having to allocate and free memory manually in the code. You can also develop graphical user interface by using Python.

Python Philosophy

In recent times, Python emerged as the leader among the established and optimized languages such as Java, C, and C++ for some straightforward reasons. It incorporates a philosophy that says that complex tasks can be done in an easy manner. We have a habit of thinking that complex, real-life problems will have complicated solutions, and the ways to go about them will be complex. The Python developers embraced a philosophy that is exactly opposite to this. It was created with the aim to have an easy learning curve which will also be quick, and the development process for the software engineers will also be fast and easy. As a result of this philosophy, Python is thought of as the best general purpose programming language, as the users of the language can work in just about any domain and still find some useful piece of code. Python was one of the flag bearers of the open source movement, and this helped it develop a massive user base from practically all modes of life. As Python is open source, people can use it to make small programs and share with each other easily. In Python, there is a group of programs for doing different tasks which is called a module or a package. When this book was written there were more than 117,181 modules submitted by a massive number of coders around the world. These large number of modules and coders have resulted in Python jumping up the ladder quickly within the computer science community and has even reached the numero uno position as the most used programming language in the world.

Python Applications

Real world applications of Python

Let's find out the actual applications of Python in the real world. In the following section of the chapter, we will go through them one by one. Before jumping into the actual coding, it helps to be able to visualize what you can do with the things you learn. You'll be able to feel the power of Python more acutely, which will provide you with the motivation to keep going. Let's begin with the Python applications.

1. Internet and Web Development: Python will allow you to develop web applications without any issues. It comes with libraries intended for internet protocol such as JSON, HTML, and XML, FTP, IMAP, e-mail processing, and simple to use socket interfaces. Still, the index of the package will show even more libraries such as:

- BeautifulSoup: HTML parser.

- Requests: HTTP client library.

- Feedparser: For parsing Atom Feeds and RSS.

- Twisted Python: For asynchronous network programming.

- Paramiko: For the implementation of the SSH2 protocol.

There is a range of frameworks available such as Pyramid and Django. Python can also provide micro frameworks such as flask and bottle. It is also possible to write CGI scripts and as a result, we can acquire advanced CMSs (Content Management Systems) such as Django CMS and Plone.

2. Desktop GUI applications of Python: Almost all the binary distributions of the programming language come with Tk, which is a standard GUI library. It empowers you to develop a user interface for your applications. Apart from that, there are other toolkits available, such as:

- Kivy, for writing the Multitouch applications

- wxWidgets

- Qt through PySide or pyqt

We can also use some toolkits which are specific to certain platforms such as Delphi, GTK+, and MS foundation classes via the win32 extension.

3. Numeric and Scientific applications: These are some of the most common applications of Python. Due to the power of Python, it is no surprise that it finds a place for itself in the scientific community. For serving this objective we have:

- **SciPy**: A collection of packages used in mathematics, engineering, and science.

- **Pandas**: This is a library used for data analysis and modeling.

- **IPython**: A powerful shell used for simple editing and works session recording. This also supports parallel computing and visualization.

- **NumPy**: Allows you to deal with complicated numerical calculations.

- **A course in software carpentry**: This advocates fundamental skills for scientific computing and for running the bootcamps. This will also provide open access teaching material.

4. Software development: Python is used as a supporting language for software development. The developers make use of Python for build-control, management, and testing as well as:

- **Buildbot/Apache Gump**: Used for automated and continuous compilation and testing.

- **SCons**: Used for build-control.

- **Roundup/Trac**: Used for tracking the bugs and project management.

- **Integrated development environment roster**: Used for displaying the comprehensive facilities provided by IDE.

5. Education applications of Python: Due to the simplicity of Python, its brevity, and large community, the programming language is a great way to be introduced to programming. There are many ways Python can be used in the field of education, and it is also possible to teach the language in schools or learn it on your own. In case you are still trying to make up your mind about Python, read on and check out its features.

6. Business applications of Python: Python is a fantastic choice for developing ERP and can also be used for e-commerce solutions. You may want to check out Tryton, which is a 3-tier, high-level general-purpose platform, or Odoo, which is a management software having several business applications. It is an all-rounder with that form and a complete suite of enterprise management applications.

7. Database access by using Python: This is one of the hottest applications of Python. By using Python, you can customize and ODBC interfaces to Oracle, MySQL, MS SQL Server, Postgre SQL, and other applications. They are available for a free download. The object databases such as ZODB and Durus along with a standard database API are also available.

8. Network Programming: Having all these possibilities included, you can pretty much expect Python to not slack in network programming. It will provide support for low-level network programming. For example:

- **Twisted Python**: A framework for asynchronous network programming.

- A simple to use socket interface is also available.

9. 3D Graphics and Games: For most people, this will be the most interesting portion of Python. Whenever someone hears that you are learning Python, the first thing you will be asked is, "Have you created a game yet?" The PyGame and PyKyra are the 2 frameworks used for game development using Python. Apart from them, you will also get a range of 3D rendering libraries. If you happen to be a game developer, you should take a look at PyWeek, which is a bi-annual game programming contest.

10. Other applications of Python: There are some other major applications of Python. Apart from those already discussed, Python will be useful in some other places as well, such as:

- Audio/video-based applications

- Image applications

- Console based applications

- Enterprise applications

- 3D Cad applications

- Machine Learning

- Artificial Intelligence

- Computer vision with facilities such as face detection or color detection

- Robotics

- Scripting

- Data analysis

As you can see, Python is everywhere, and now that you are aware of its applications, you know when to use it. It makes a programmer feel more powerful than ever before. Even more unique projects can be made by using Python as the programming language.

Some Shortcomings of Python

By the year 2015, Python had become one of the most globally used programming languages. In addition to being easy-to-learn and simple, it empowers the coders to express the code without having to write long lines. Its easy syntax together with the readable code makes it simple to maintain the applications written in Python. The robust standard library and many such advantages can be associated with Python. However, like all other programming languages, Python has some shortcomings as well. As a programmer, it is important to know the major limitations of Python. Here are the main ones:

1. Speed and performance: Several studies conducted have conclusively proven that Python is slower than its counterparts, such as C++ and Java. As a result, coders have to constantly explore methods for enhancing the speed of Python applications. But, you have some options to enable the applications in Python to run faster. For example, coders can specify a custom runtime and make use of it, rather than the default runtime used in the programming language. Similarly, they may rewrite the existing code in Python for taking advantage of the current execution speed.

2. Incompatibility between the two versions: Many times, beginners have to pick one of the available versions to learn Python. Actually, the second version of Python is described as legacy and the third as futuristic. However, both versions of the programming language are updated on a regular basis. There are a massive number of programmers out there who still prefer 2nd version rather than the current 3rd. You can also find a number of libraries and frameworks supporting just Python 2.

3. Portability of applications: This is a high-level language and as a result, interpreters are required by the developers to convert the Python code into something understandable to the operating system. You are required to install specific versions of Python interpreters on the OS for running Python applications on the platform. This disadvantage prevents programmers from using Python cross-platform in application development. Also, it is not possible to port the applications from one platform to another easily.

4. Additional testing is required: This is a dynamic type of programming language. Python doesn't need the developers to define the variable type when they are declaring it. This feature makes it easy for programmers to write the code freely.

However, a number of critical defects will come up during compilation as the type of variables is not defined explicitly. Therefore, the programmers have to perform a number of extra tests for identifying and fixing the defects during runtime.

5. Lack of web development capabilities: Although several developers like to use Python as a scripting language for building web applications quickly, Python does not come with a built-in web development facility. Another problem is that the standard implementation of Python doesn't bolster the performance of web applications across several browsers. This is the reason why the developers make use of several web frameworks from Python, in addition to improving the effectiveness of web application development. But they have the option of selecting from a range of web frameworks for Python including TurboGear, web2py, Zope2, Reahland, and Django.

6. Not good at mobile computing: The continuous decline in the use of internet on mobiles forced modern businesses to launch a series of mobile apps. The developers are often required to write mobile apps in a specific language as per targeted the mobile platform. For example, the coder will write the iOS app in either Swift or Objective-C. Similarly, mobile apps for Android have to be written in Java. However, the developers can't use this language directly for the development of mobile apps by targeting popular mobile platforms. They must use frameworks such as Kivy for building cross-platform mobile apps by using Python.

7. Dependence of 3rd party libraries and frameworks: Python does not include many of the features provided by other programming languages. Therefore, programmers have to use a number of 3rd party tools and frameworks for building web applications and mobile apps in Python. But they have to use an open source framework and libraries to avoid rising project overheads. The use of advanced features and functionalities supplied by the commercial framework is restricted due to the cost factor.

8. Embedding block comments are not possible: These days, it is mandatory for the developers to make the code used in the application to be maintainable and readable. While writing the code, programmers many at times deactivate the specific sections of a block of code with the use of block comments. Unlike other programming languages used these days, Python does not support block commenting. Therefore, the developers have to assess the code quality either by writing the comments for every code line or by removing specific sections of code during the execution time. Lack of this support of block comments means the programmers need to place additional effort and time in assessing Python code quality.

9. No adequate support for several modules: Python is endorsed by a massive and active community. Members of the community constantly share new modules or packages for making things easier for the programmers to add functionality to their apps. However, the programmers many times complain that there is a difference in the quality of various Python modules. Many of these packages lack adequate support and do not get updated constantly. Therefore programmers are forced to perform some research initially for picking the right modules and packages.

10. Prior built statistical models and tests are not provided: There are several programmers out there who prefer to use Python for developing customized statistical and big data apps. However, the developers have to use some extra data analysis and statistical packages for writing statistical applications better. And they are forced to use specific libraries such as Seaborn, Pygal, and Bokeh for accomplishing the data visualization. It is not possible to get the Python application to present and analyze the massive volume of data without making use of the tools and libraries.

All-in-all, programmers may use Python for building a range of software applications quickly, however, it is essential to use several 3rd party frameworks and libraries in addition to those provided by Python to overcome the shortcomings of the high-level language. Also, it is necessary to find ways of enhancing the speed and performance of Python applications reliably.

Chapter 2: Python Programming Tips for Beginners

One of the most common queries when candidates embark on the journey to learn Python is, "What is the best method for learning Python?" Well, the first step towards learning Python is understanding how to learn it. It is vital to know the best methods for learning any computer programming related lessons. This is because as the programming languages evolve, new libraries are created and its tools get upgraded. Knowing the learning process is essential for keeping up with the changes and keeping yourself updated as a programmer. Here are some learning strategies which will jump start you towards becoming a rock star programmer of Python:

1. Keep coding each day

Consistency is of paramount importance when you are learning a new programming language. It is recommended that you make a commitment to writing the code each day. Although it is hard to believe that muscle memory will play a big part in programming, commitment to writing the code each day really helps in developing that muscle memory. It does sound a bit heavy at first, but go for smaller chunks every day - for, say, 25 minutes, and then work your way up from there. There is plenty of help available here in this book and online for getting you started.

2. Write down notes every day

As you make headway as a new developer, you will start feeling the need to take down some notes. Yes, it is a good idea. As a matter of fact, the research suggests that taking down notes by hand is extremely beneficial towards long term retention in your mind. It will be extremely useful for those who are planning on becoming full-time developers. Remember, most interviews will involve writing down the code on whiteboards.

When you begin working on smaller programs and projects, this habit of writing down with hands helps you in planning your code before moving on to the PC. It saves a great deal of time when you can write down what classes you will need along with the functions and also how they can interact.

3. Be interactive

It doesn't matter whether you are learning about fundamental Python data structures such as lists, strings, and dictionaries for the first time, or you are debugging some application - this interactive Python shell is one of the better learning tools. It is used a lot on the internet. To use the interactive Python shell, which is also referred to as Python REPL at times, first ensure that Python is installed on your computer. There is a step-by-step tutorial available to aid you with that. For activating the interactive Python shell, all you need to do is open the terminal and run the Python version specific to the installation. Some detailed directions are also available online for this.

Now that you know about starting a shell, here are some examples of using the shell for learning Python:

Learn about the operations which can be performed on an element with the use of dir():

```
>>> my_string = 'I am a string'
```

```
>>> dir(my_string)
```

```
['__add__', ..., 'upper', 'zfill']  # Truncated for readability
```

Elements that are returned from the dri() are the methods you may apply to that element. For instance:

```
>>> my_string.upper()
>>> 'I AM A STRING'
```

Make a note here that we called the method upper(). Can you guess what it will do? It will make all the letters of the string upper case. There are built-in methods to be found on Python, and you can learn about them elsewhere. Now learn about the type of the element.

```
>>> type(my_string)
>>> str
```

You can use the built-in help system for getting full documentation like this:

```
>>> help(str)
```

You may import the libraries and work with them by:

```
>>> from datetime import datetime
>>> dir(datetime)
['__add__', ..., 'weekday', 'year']  # Truncated for readability
```

>>> datetime.now()

datetime.datetime(2018, 3, 14, 23, 44, 50, 851904)

You may run the shell commands with:

>>> import os

>>> os.system('ls')

python_hw1.py python_hw2.py README.txt[1]

4. Take a few breaks

While you are learning, it is vital to step away from the process at times and grip the concepts you have learned. One widely used technique for this is the Pomodoro technique, which can help in the process. Using this technique, you exert effort for 25 minutes and then take a small break and reiterate the procedure. Taking these breaks is important during intense study sessions, typically when you are consuming a lot of new info. These breaks are especially important while debugging. If you run into a defect and are not sure how to find out what is going wrong, take some time out. Step away from the desk and go for a walk or talk to a friend. While using any programming language, it is mandatory that your code follows the rules of the language and logic perfectly, so if you even miss a quotation mark, it might break something. Coming back to it with a fresh pair of eyes will make a huge difference.

---

[1] Krishelle Hardson-Hurley. 11 Beginner Tips for Learning Python Programming. (2018). https://realpython.com/python-beginner-tips/

5. Turn into a bounty hunter of bugs

Running into bugs is pretty much inevitable when you begin with writing complex programs by using the codes. It happens to everyone. Do not allow the bugs to frustrate you. Rather, embrace these moments with open eyes and consider yourself as the bounty hunter of bugs. It is important to have a methodical approach while debugging, as it is critical for finding out where things will break down. Going through the code in its execution order and making sure that every part of it is working as it should is the best way of doing this. When you realize where the things are breaking down, add the following lines of code in the script:

```
import pdb; pdb.set_trace()
```

Then run the script. This is the Python debugger, and will take you to the interactive mode. The debugger will also be run from command lines with

```
python -m pdb <my_file.py>
```

Once things have started to stick, make a collaborative effort to expedite learning. The following strategies are useful to get the most out of working with the others.

6. Be with people who are learning as well

Although coding looks like an isolated activity, it always works better when you are working together. It's extremely helpful while you are learning to code in Python language that you are surrounding yourself with other learners who are going through the same phase as well. It allows you to share the tricks and the tips of learning during the process. However, do not worry if you don't know of anyone who is also learning at the same time. There are many ways of meeting other people who are passionate about Python learning, like yourself. You can look for meetups or local events, or join pythonistaCafe, which is a peer-to-peer learning community for the Python enthusiasts such as yourself.

7. Try to teach others what you have learned

It is often told that the best way of learning something is to teach it to others. This is true for learning Python, as well. You can do this in several ways, such as whiteboarding with other Python users, writing blog posts about newly learned concepts, recording videos which will explain things that you have learned, or just talking to yourself when sitting at your desk. All these ways will improve your understanding of the language and expose the gaps, if there are any, in your understanding.

8. Pair programming

This is a technique which involves 2 programmers working on a single workstation for completing a task. These 2 programmers switch between the roles of driver and navigator. The driver will write the Python code, while the navigator will aid in problem-solving and reviewing the code as it is being written. They will switch constantly to achieve the benefits of using both sides. Pair programming has several benefits. It allows each individual a chance to not just have someone reviewing their code, but also to have someone around whose views about the problem at hand can be useful. Getting exposed to multiple ideas and methods of thinking will help in problem-solving once you get back to coding on your own.

9. Ask all the good questions

People often say that there is no such thing as a bad question. However, when you are looking to learn to program, it is likely that you may ask a bad question. For example, when you are asking for help from people who are not in sync with the problem you are facing, it is a better idea to ask good questions using this acronym:

G: Give the right context on the problem by describing what you are doing.

O: Outline everything you have done to fix the issue you are facing.

O: Offer the best guess about what the issue is. It aids the person that is helping you to understand what you are thinking and also will help them to know that you have done some thinking of your own as well.

D: Demonstrate what the problem is. Include the traceback error message, the code you have written, and provide an explanation about the steps you performed which resulted in the error you are getting. With this method, the person who is helping out doesn't have to try and recreate the problems you are facing.

These good questions will save a lot of your time. By skipping any of the steps, you will get tangled into many back-and-forth conversations which may cause conflict. When you are a beginner, you should ensure that you are asking the good questions. This is because as you practice communication with your thought process and people that are trying to help, you want them to be happy to keep on helping you!

Almost all the developers of Python you speak to will let you know that when learning Python, you must do it yourself.

Performing exercises and viewing tutorials will only carry you so far. You need to start from the ground up to learn the language in depth.

10. Just go on and build something, anything will do

For the Python beginners, there are several small exercises available which will aid you in becoming confident with the programming language and develop your muscle memory as discussed above. When you have a total grasp of the fundamental data structures such as lists, strings, sets, dictionaries, writing classes, and OOP, it is time you start building. It is not important what you build, but how you do it is. The whole process of building will teach you many things. You will learn only so much by reading Python articles and courses. Almost all of your learning will come by using the language to build things and the issues you will resolve. The process will teach you quite a bit. There are several lists of ideas out there for beginner projects for Python users. Here are a few for getting you started:

- Basic calculator app

- Number guessing game

- Bitcoin price notification service

- Dice roll simulator

You can find many more project ideas online for practice if you are stuck.

11. Contribute towards the open source software

The source code of the software is available publicly in case of an open source model, and anyone may contribute towards it. You can find many Python libraries which are open source projects that can accept contributions. In addition to this, several organizations publish open-source projects. This means that you can see and work with the code written by engineers working in the professional atmosphere of these companies. Contributing to the Python open source projects is a fantastic way of creating valuable learning experiences. Let's say you want to submit a request for bug fixing. You will submit "pull request" for the fix, which will be patched in your code.

The project managers will review the work next and provide suggestions and comments. This will help you learn about the best practices for programming in Python, and you will get the practice of communicating with other programmers. For more tricks and tips which will aid you in making grounds in this world of open source software, look for videos on the web.

Chapter 3: Python Language Syntax and Semantics

Python programming language was actually developed for teaching purposes. However, its ease of use with a clean syntax led to it being used by beginners and connoisseurs alike. As a matter of fact, the cleanliness of Python syntax has led to people calling it "executable pseudocode." The people who have used it conform to the fact that Python scripting is a lot easier to read and comprehend than similar scripts are written in C. Now let's begin a discussion on the important features of the Python syntax. The syntax means the language structure, i.e. what will mean a correctly formatted program. Let's not concentrate on semantics, which deals with the meaning of symbols and words in the syntax. However, we will return to it sometime later. Now, let's consider a sample code for instance:

```python
# set the midpoint

midpoint = 5

# make two empty lists

lower = []; upper = []

# split the numbers into lower and upper

for i in range(10):

    if (i < midpoint):

        lower.append(i)
```

```
else:

    upper.append(i)

print("lower:", lower)

print("upper:", upper)

lower: [0, 1, 2, 3, 4]

upper: [5, 6, 7, 8, 9]
```
[2]

It is a lame script, arguably, but displays many significant aspects of Python syntax compactly. Let us walk through the program and check out the syntactical features of the programming language.

This program's script starts with the comment:

```
# set the midpoint
```

All comments of Python are marked by a # sign, and the things that follow the # sign are ignored by the interpreter. For instance, it means that you can have stand-alone comments such as the one displayed apart from the inline comments which follow the statement. For instance:

```
x += 2  # shorthand for x = x + 2
```

_____

[2] A Quick Tour of Python Language Syntax.
https://jakevdp.github.io/WhirlwindTourOfPython/02-basic-python-syntax.html

Python will not have a syntax for comments that have several lines like /* ... */. This is a kind of syntax used for C and C++, although multiline strings are normally used as replacements for the multiline comments. The next line of your script is:

midpoint = 5

It is an assignment operation in which a variable called midpoint has been created and has been assigned a value of 5. Make a note here that the end of the statement is marked just by the end of the line. It is a direct contrast to other programming languages such as C and C++, in which all the statements have to end with ";" (a semicolon). In case you wish to get the statement to continue to the next line in Python, you may use the "\" marker for indicating this. For instance:

x = 1 + 2 + 3 + 4 +\

5 + 6 + 7 + 8

You can also continue with having expressions on the next line inside a parenthesis without having to use the "\" marker. For instance:

x = (1 + 2 + 3 + 4 +

    5 + 6 + 7 + 8)

The style guides for Python will recommend the 2nd version for line continuation mostly (that is, having it within parenthesis) rather than the first (by using the "\" mark).

The semicolon is capable of terminating a statement optionally, as it can be useful for putting multiple statements in a single line. The next portion of your script goes like this:

```
lower = []; upper = []
```

It displays an example of how a semicolon used commonly in C can be utilized in Python for placing 2 statements in one line. Functionally, it is equivalent to writing the code like this:

```
lower = []
upper = []
```

Most of the Python style guides will discourage the use of semicolon for placing multiple statements in a single line, although at times it proves to be remarkably convenient.

Indentation is important in Python, as the whitespace is significant. Let's go to the main code block.

```
for i in range(10):
    if i < midpoint:
        lower.append(i)
```

else:

upper.append(i)[3]

This is a control flow statement which is compound and includes a condition and a loop. We will take a look at these kinds of statements later. At the moment, just remember that this demonstrates probably the most controversial feature of the Python syntax, and that is meaningful whitespaces. In any programming language, a set of code must be treated as a unit. For example, in C the code chunks are designated by curly braces.

```c
// C code
for(int i=0; i<100; i++)

  {

    // curly braces indicate code block

    total += i;

  }
```

The code blocks in Python are represented by using indentation.

```python
for i in range(100):

  # indentation indicates code block
```

---

[3] A Quick Tour of Python Language Syntax.
https://jakevdp.github.io/WhirlwindTourOfPython/02-basic-python-syntax.html

total += i[4]

The indented code sets in Python will be preceded by a colon in the previous line. The indentation helps to enforce a readable and uniform style, which several people find to be the most appealing part of the Python code. However, it is confusing for the uninitiated. Let's look at the following code, for example. These 2 snippets will provide 2 different results.

```
>>> if x < 4:        >>> if x < 4:
...    y = x * 2     ...    y = x * 2
...    print(x)      ... print(x)[5]
```

In the first snippet on the left, the print(x) statement is in the indented set and will get executed only in case x happens to be less than 4. The snippet on the right which is also print(x) is out of the block and gets executed with no influence of the x value.

The utilization of meaningful whitespaces by Python has often

---

[4] A Quick Tour of Python Language Syntax.
https://jakevdp.github.io/WhirlwindTourOfPython/02-basic-python-syntax.html

[5] A Quick Tour of Python Language Syntax.
https://jakevdp.github.io/WhirlwindTourOfPython/02-basic-python-syntax.html

been a surprise for several programmers who are used to other programming languages, but the truth of the matter is that it leads to a much more reliable and legible code compared to other languages which do not use code block indentation.

In case you find the use of whitespaces to be uncomfortable, give it a try first. You might actually come to appreciate it. And lastly, the amount of whitespace utilized for indentation of the code blocks is up to the code user so long as it is consistent in the script. Most of the style guides by convention recommend the use of indented code blocks up to 4 spaces. That convention is followed in the examples cited here. Keep in mind that several text editors such as Vim and Emacs contain Python modes which will do the 4 space indentation automatically.

However, remember that the whitespacing within the lines does not matter. Although the convention of meaningful whitespaces will hold its ground for whitespaces before the lines of a code block, the whitespaces existing within the Python code lines do not matter. For instance, all these expressions are equivalent:

```
x=1+2

x = 1 + 2

x        =    1 +           2
```

If you abuse the offered flexibility, it will lead to code readability problems. As a matter of fact, abusing the whitespaces is many times the main means of obfuscating the code intentionally, and some people do it for playing with the code. Use of whitespaces will lead to a far more readable code, especially in places where there are operators following each other. Let's check out the 2 following expressions for exponentiation with negative numbers.

x=10**-2

and

x = 10 ** -2

You will find that the second line is more easily readable with spaces at a glance. Almost all the Python style guides will recommend the use of single spacing around binary operators, and there should not be any space around unary operators.

Parentheses are used for calling or grouping. In the previous example of Python code, we would have observed 2 uses of parentheses. Firstly, they will be used in a common way of grouping statements or mathematical operations. For example:

In: 2 * (3 + 4)

Out: 14

These braces are also used for indicating that a function is called. In your next snippet, you will find the function print() being used to show the variable content. Check out the sidebar. The call to a function is indicated by the pair of closing and opening braces and the function arguments are contained within the parentheses.

```
print('first value:', 1)
```

```
first value: 1
```

```
print('second value:', 2)
```

```
second value: 2
```

Many functions are called without any arguments at all in it. But the opening and closing parentheses must be used for indicating the evaluation of a function. One common example of this is a sort method of lists.

```
L = [4,2,3,1]
```

```
L.sort()
```

```
print(L)
```

```
[1, 2, 3, 4]
```

The parentheses coming after the "sort" indicate that this function must be executed although the parentheses contain no arguments within them.

Let's now look at an important note for using the print() function. We used the print() function above as an example. But this function happens to be the one item that has changed in between the transition from Python 2.x to Python 3.x. In the 2nd version, the print() worked as a statement. So, you could write:

```
# Python 2 only!

>> print "first value:", 1

first value: 1
```

But for a range of reasons, the keepers of Python decided that they would use print() as a function in Python 3. Therefore now we write like this:

```
# Python 3 only!

>>> print("first value:", 1)

first value: 1
```

It happens to be one of the several incompatible constructs existing between the second and the third versions of Python. When this book was being written it was common to find the examples written in both Python versions and the print being used as a statement rather than as a function. They are many times the first indications that you are looking at the Python 2 code and not the Python 3 code.

Summary

These are some of the brief and essential features used in Python syntax. It is intended to provide a good reference point when you read more about the Python code later in the book.

Here there is a reference to style guide which helps in writing code in a consistent manner. You can find the most commonly used style guide as PEP8 for Python online. As you will become more proficient in writing the Python code, it will be useful to go through it. This style guide has contributions from many gurus of Python, and most suggestions will go beyond the straightforward pedantry. These recommendations are based on experience and will be useful in avoiding subtle mistakes and issues within the code.

Fundamental Python Semantics

Variables and Objects

In this section, we will cover the fundamental semantics of the Python programming language. Contrary to the syntax we covered in the previous section, semantics of a programming language are related to the meanings of statements. Similar to the description about the Python syntax, here we will see some important semantic constructions used in Python for giving you a better reference frame to understand the code in upcoming sections. The chapter will cover the semantics of objects and variables which happen to be the main methods of storing, referencing, and operating on the data in a Python script.

Variables as pointers: In Python, assigning the variables is extremely simple - in fact, you just have to place the variable name on the left of the equals (=) sign.

assign 4 to the variable x

x = 4

It might appear straightforward, but if you have an incorrect mental model of the output of this operation, Python will appear confusing to you. We will dig into it a bit here. In several programming languages, the variables are considered as containers or buckets for placing your data. Therefore, in the case of C language for instance, if you write:

```
// C code

int x = 4;
```

you will be defining a memory bucket called "x," essentially, and placing the value 4 in it. However, in Python, the variables are at best considered not as containers but as pointers. Therefore in Python when you have written:

x = 4

You will be defining a pointer called x which points to another bucket containing the value of 4. Make a note of a consequence of this. As the Python variables only point to different objects, there just isn't any need for declaring the variable or the requirement that a variable must point to the info of similar type. It is in this sense that people comment that the language is dynamically typed. The variable names will point to objects of any kind. Therefore you may do things like these in Python:

```
x = 1      # x is an integer

x = 'hello'  # now x is a string

x = [1, 2, 3] # now x is a list
```

Although the users of the statistically-typed programming languages may actually miss the type-safety which is associated with the declarations as those found in C:

```
int x = 4;
```

The dynamic typing is one of the pieces which make Python very fast to write and simple to read. There are consequences to having this variable to pointer approach which you must be aware of. If we have 2 variable names pointing to the exact same mutable object, then changing one can change the other as well. For instance, let's create and modify one list:

```
x = [1, 2, 3]

y = x
```

Here there are 2 variables, x and y, and they point to the same object. Due to this, if we modify this list through one of the names, we can find that the other list gets modified also.

```
print(y)
```

```
[1, 2, 3]
```

```
x.append(4) # append 4 to the list pointed to by x
```

```
print(y) # y's list is modified as well!
```

```
[1, 2, 3, 4]
```

This behavior will appear confusing if you are incorrectly thinking of variables as buckets which contain data. However, if you are properly thinking of them as pointers to objects, then all of this will make perfect sense. Make a note here that we are using "=" for assigning a value to x. It will not affect the value of y. Here, assignment is only changing what the object of the variable is pointing to.

```
x = 'something else'
```

```
print(y)  # y is unchanged
```

```
[1, 2, 3, 4]
```

This will again make a perfect sense if you consider x and y to be pointers and the "=" operator to be an operation which changes what the name is pointing to. One thing that springs to the mind is, "Does this pointer business make arithmetic operations difficult to keep track of in Python?" However, Python is set in such a fashion that this is not a problem. Strings, numbers, and other simple types cannot be muted, so it is not possible to change their value. You may only change the values that the variable is pointing to. Therefore, for instance, it is totally safe to perform operations such as these:

x = 10

y = x

x += 5 # add 5 to x's value, and assign it to x

print("x =", x)

print("y =", y)

x = 15

y = 10^6

If we call x+=5, we will not be modifying the object 10 pointed to with x, but we are instead changing the variable x so that it will point to a new integer object having value 15. Due to these reasons, the y value is not affected by this operation.

In Python, everything will be an object: It is an Object Oriented Programming language, so everything in Python will be an object. Let's understand what this means. In an earlier part of the discussion, we saw that variables in Python are nothing but pointers, and the variable names have no attached kind of info. It leads to some claims which are incorrect - that this is a type-free language. That is not true. Now, take a look

---

[6] *Jake VanderPlas*. Basic Python Semantics: Variables and Objects. https://jakevdp.github.io/WhirlwindTourOfPython/03-semantics-variables.html

at the following:

x = 4

type(x)

int

x = 'hello'

type(x)

str

x = 3.14159

type(x)

float

So, Python does have types, but they are not linked to the variable names. Instead, they are linked to the object itself. In any OOP language such as Python, objects will be an entity which contains data with the associated metadata and the functionality. As we know in Python, everything is an object, and this means all entities have some metadata called attributes and the related functionality called methods. These methods and attributes are accessed by using the dot syntax. Before looking at the lists, keep an append method which will add an item to your list that gets accessed through the dot syntax.

For instance, before we became aware that the lists have one append method that adds an item to a list and gets accesses through the dot "." syntax.

```
L = [1, 2, 3]

L.append(100)

print(L)

[1, 2, 3, 100]
```

Although it is expected for the compound objects such as lists to have methods and attributes, what can be unexpected is that in Python, the easy types come with attached methods and attributes. For instance, the numerical types have real and img attributes which return real and imaginary part of this value in the case viewed as some complex number.

```
x = 4.5

print(x.real, "+", x.imag, 'i')

4.5 + 0.0 I
```

The methods are similar to attributes except for the fact that they are functions you may call by using the opening and closing digressions. For instance, the floating point numbers come with a method called is_integer, which checks if a value is an integer.

```
x = 4.5

x.is_integer()

False
```

x = 4.0

x.is_integer()

True

Once we comment that everything in Python is an object, it is intended that "everything" is an object. Even the methods and attributes of objects are also objects themselves having their own type info.

type(x.is_integer)

builtin_function_or_method

We can observe that the design type of Python which is "everything is object" permits some very useful language constructs.

Operators

In an earlier section of the chapter, we took a look at the semantics of variables and objects of Python. Now, let's consider the semantics of different operators included in Python. By the time you are through with this section, you will have gained access to the fundamental tools to start comparing the operators on the data in Python.

Arithmetic Operations

There are 7 fundamental binary operators in Python, two of which can be used as unary operators. These operators are abridged in this table:

Operator	Name	Description
a + b	Addition	Sum of a and b
a - b	Subtraction	Difference of a and b
a * b	Multiplication	Product of a and b
a / b	True division	Quotient of a and b
a // b	Floor division	Quotient of a and b, removing fractional parts
a % b	Modulus	Integer remainder after division of a by b
a ** b	Exponentiation	a raised to the power of b
-a	Negation	The negative of a
+a	Unary plus	a unchanged (rarely used)[7]

The operators mentioned above may be used in several intuitive ways by using standard parentheses to group operations. For instance:

---

[7] *Jake VanderPlas.* Basic Python Semantics: Operators.
https://jakevdp.github.io/WhirlwindTourOfPython/04-semantics-operators.html

addition, subtraction, multiplication

(4 + 8) * (6.5 - 3)

42.0

Floor division is a true division by using the fractional parts which are truncated.

True division

print(11 / 2)

5.5

Floor division

print(11 // 2)

5

Your floor division operator was a new addition to Python 3. In case you are working in Python 2, you must be aware that your standard division operator will act as floor division for the integers and similar to a true division for the floating point numbers. Keep in mind the 8th arithmetic operator which was added to Python 3.5 and it is a@b operator. This is meant to indicate the matrix product of a and b. It is to be used in different linear algebra packages.

Bitwise operations

Apart from the standard numerical operations, this programming language includes the operators for performing bitwise logical operations on the integers. These operators are not generally used much compared to the standard arithmetic operators. However, it is great to know that they are there.

There are six bitwise operators, and they are described in this table:

Operator	Name	Description
a & b	Bitwise AND	Bits defined in both a and b
a | b	Bitwise OR	Bits defined in a or b or both
a ^ b	Bitwise XOR	Bits defined in a or b but not both
a << b	Bit shift left	Shift bits of a left by b units
a >> b	Bit shift right	Shift bits of a right by b units
~a	Bitwise NOT	Bitwise negation of a[8]

The bitwise operators will only make nous in terms of numbers' binary representation. You can see this while using the bin (built-in) function.

bin(10)

'0b1010'

The result of the code is prefixed with '0b' and it indicates binary representation. The remaining digits indicate that 10 the number is expressed as a sum:

---

[8] *Jake VanderPlas*. Basic Python Semantics: Operators.
https://jakevdp.github.io/WhirlwindTourOfPython/04-semantics-operators.html

$1.2^3 + 0.2^2 + 1.2^1 + 0.2^0$

Like this, we may write:

bin(4)

'0b100'

We can use the bitwise OR for finding out the number which blends the bits 4 and 10.

4 | 10

14

bin(4 | 10)

'0b1110'

Although the bitwise operators are not as directly useful as the arithmetic operators, it will be useful to known them and understand what class of operations they will perform. Specifically, the users of other programming languages are many times tempted to use XOR i.e. a ^ b while what they really intend is exponentiation {i.e. a**b}.

Assignment Operations

So far we have learned that the variables can be assigned a "=" operator and its values may be stored for use later. For instance:

```
a = 24

print(a)

24
```

These variables can be used in various expressions, along with the operators described earlier. For instance, for adding 2 to an "a" we will write:

```
a + 2

26
```

Here we may wish to add a new value to the variable a. For example, we might want to combine addition and assignment and write a = a + 2. As this kind of combination of assigning and adding is very common, Python has the built-in updating operators for use during arithmetic operations.

```
a += 2  # equivalent to a = a + 2

print(a)

26
```

You can find an augmented assignment operator coinciding with every one of the binary operators which are listed earlier. Briefly speaking these are:

a += b   a -= b   a *= b   a /= b

a //= b   a %= b   a **= b   a &= b

a |= b   a ^= b   a <<= b   a >>= b[9]

Every one of them is equivalent to the subsequent operation and is then followed by the assignment. This means for any operator "x", your expression a x= b happens to be equivalent to a = a x b - but there is a catch here. For the mutable objects such as arrays, lists, or dataframes, the augmented assignment operators will act subtly different compared to their more verbose counterparts. These operators change the original object contents instead of creating new objects for storing the results.

Comparison Operations

There is another kind of operation which is extremely useful, and that is a comparison of different values. For the purpose Python will implement standard comparison operators that will return Boolean values viz. True and False. These comparison operations are listed here:

---

[9] *Jake VanderPlas.* Basic Python Semantics: Operators.
https://jakevdp.github.io/WhirlwindTourOfPython/04-semantics-operators.html

Operation	Description	Operation	Description
a == b	a equal to b	a != b	a not equal to b
a < b	a less than b	a > b	a greater than b
a <= b	a less than or equal to b	a >= b	a greater than or equal to b [10]

The comparison operations are blended with bitwise and arithmetic operations in order to express a practically unlimited range of tests for your numbers. For instance, we may check whether some number is odd by checking if the modulus of 2 will return 1:

25 is odd

25 % 2 == 1

True

66 is odd

66 % 2 == 1

False

We may string together several comparisons for checking the more complicated relationships:

---

[10] *Jake VanderPlas*. Basic Python Semantics: Operators.
https://jakevdp.github.io/WhirlwindTourOfPython/04-semantics-operators.html

check if a is between 15 and 30

a = 25

15 < a < 30

True

Let's see a bit more taxing part. See this comparison:

-1 == ~0

True[11]

In case you have forgotten, the ~ is a bit-flip operator and apparently, when you flip the bits of zero, you will end up with a -1. If you are curious about why this is so, have a look at the "two's complement" scheme for integer encoding used by Python for encoding signed integers, and think about what will happen when you start flipping the integer bits encoded in this manner.

Boolean Operations

Python, while working with the Boolean values, will ask the operators to blend the values by using standard concepts such as "And", "Not", and "Or." Obviously, the operators are stated by using the words and, not, and or, like this:

---

[11] A Quick Tour of Python Language Syntax. (2016). https://jakevdp.github.io/WhirlwindTourOfPython/02-basic-python-syntax.html

x = 4

(x < 6) and (x > 2)

True

(x > 10) or (x % 2 == 0)

True

not (x < 6)

False[12]

Those who are experts in Boolean algebra will note here that their XOR operator will not be encompassed here. It may be constructed in many ways, though, from the compound statements of the other operators. Alternatively, there is a clever trick you may use for the XOR of Boolean value, and that is:

(x > 1) xor (x < 10)

(x > 1) != (x < 10)

False

These kinds of Boolean operations are very useful when you start talking about the control flow statements like the loops

---

[12] A Quick Tour of Python Language Syntax. (2016). https://jakevdp.github.io/WhirlwindTourOfPython/02-basic-python-syntax.html

and conditionals. One of the uncertainties many face is not knowing when to use the Boolean operators and, not, and or, and when to go for the bitwise operators |, ~, and &. The answer to this problem lies in the names of the operators. When you wish to calculate the Boolean values of the full statements, the Boolean operators have to be used, i.e. true or false. Similarly, the bitwise operators must be used when you wish to operate on independent bits and components of the objects in question.

Membership and Identity operators

Python, similar to the "And", "Not", and "Or," also has operators similar to prose for checking the membership and identity. These operators are used like this:

Operator   Description

a is b   True if a and b are identical objects

a is not b   True if a and b are not identical objects

a in b   True if a is a member of b

a not in b   True if a is not a member of b[13]

Identity operators "is" and "is not"

These identity operators which are "is" and "is not" will check for object identity. Remember that equality is different from object identity. Let's see an example of this:

---

[13] A Quick Tour of Python Language Syntax. (2016). https://jakevdp.github.io/WhirlwindTourOfPython/02-basic-python-syntax.html

```
a = [1, 2, 3]
```

```
b = [1, 2, 3]
```

```
a == b
```

True

```
a is b
```

False

```
a is not b
```

True

Now let's look at the example of what the identical objects appear as:

```
a = [1, 2, 3]
```

```
b = a
```

```
a is b
```

True[14]

Here, the variance between the two cases is that in the first, a and b will point to different objects, and in the second they will point to the same object. As observed in the previous section,

---

[14] A Quick Tour of Python Language Syntax. (2016). https://jakevdp.github.io/WhirlwindTourOfPython/02-basic-python-syntax.html

all Python variables are pointers. The "is" operator will check whether both the variables are pointing to the same container or object instead of referring to the content of the container. Keeping this in mind - in almost all the cases, a beginner is tempted to utilize "is." What that really indicates to is ==.

Membership operators

These membership operators will check for membership in compound objects. Therefore, for instance, we may write:

1 in [1, 2, 3]

True

2 not in [1, 2, 3]

False

The membership operators are a good example of what makes Python simple to use compared to other lower-level languages like C. While using C, the membership is normally determined by manual construction of loops over the lists and checking for equality of every value. In Python, you can go on and type what you wish to know, which is similar to the English prose.

Control Flow Statements

This is where you really must be at your best while programming. Without control flow, a program is just a list of statements which get executed sequentially. By using the control flow, you become capable of executing certain code blocks conditionally and if required repeatedly. The fundamental building blocks may be blended together to develop some shockingly sophisticated programs. In this section, we will cover the conditional statements such as "if", "else-if", and "else." We will also cover loop statements such as "for" and "while" with the "continue", "break", and "pass."

Conditional statements

These statements viz. if-elif-else are often referred to as the if-then statements. They allow the user to execute some pieces of code according to a certain Boolean condition. A fundamental example of the Python conditional statements is:

```
x = -15

if x == 0:

    print(x, "is zero")

elif x > 0:

    print(x, "is positive")

elif x < 0:

    print(x, "is negative")

else:

    print(x, "is unlike anything I've ever seen...")

-15 is negative
```
[15]

---

[15] *Jake VanderPlas.* Basic Python Semantics: Control flow. (2016).

Here make a note of the colon use (:) and whitespaces for denoting separate code blocks. Python will adopt the "if" and "else" normally used in other programming languages. The more unique keyword is "elif" which is a contracted form of else if. Among the conditional clauses, the blocks containing elif and else are optional. In addition to that, you may also include as many elif statements as you wish.

For Loops

In Python, the "For" loops are ways of executing the code statement repeatedly. Therefore, for instance, if you wish to print every item in a list, you may use a "for" loop for the purpose. For example:

```
for N in [2, 3, 5, 7]:

    print(N, end=' ') # print all on same line

2 3 5 7 [16]
```

Make a note of the simplicity of the loop here. You just specify the variable you wish to use along with sequence you wish to loop over and utilize the "in" operator for linking them together

---

https://jakevdp.github.io/WhirlwindTourOfPython/07-control-flow-statements.html

[16] *Jake VanderPlas*. Basic Python Semantics: Control flow. (2016). https://jakevdp.github.io/WhirlwindTourOfPython/07-control-flow-statements.html

in readable and intuitive ways. The object on the right side of "in" will be the iterator of Python. The iterator can be thought of as a generalized sequence. For instance, one of the commonly utilized interpreters of Python is the range object that generates a sequence of numbers. For instance:

```
for i in range(10):

    print(i, end=' ')

0 1 2 3 4 5 6 7 8 9
```

Here, as you can see, the range starts at 0 by default. According to the convention, the top value of the range is not included in the displayed output. The range objects may also have some complex values such as:

```
# range from 5 to 10

list(range(5, 10))

[5, 6, 7, 8, 9]

# range from 0 to 10 by 2

list(range(0, 10, 2))

[0, 2, 4, 6, 8][17]
```

---

[17] *Jake VanderPlas.* Control Flow. (2016).
https://jakevdp.github.io/WhirlwindTourOfPython/07-control-flow-statements.html

One might remember that the range argument meaning is similar to the slicing syntax covered in the Lists. Keep in mind here that the behavior of Range() is one of the main differences between Python 2 and 3. In "2" the Range() will produce a list while in "3" the Range() will produce iterable objects.

While Loops

There is another kind of loop available for use in Python, and that is While loop. It will iterate until some of the conditions are met.

```
i = 0

while i < 10:

    print(i, end=' ')

    i += 1

0 1 2 3 4 5 6 7 8 9
```

The arguments in the While loop are evaluated as Boolean statements, and the loop will be executed until the statement evaluation becomes false.

Break and Continue: Fine-tuning the loops

You can find 2 useful statements which may be used within the loops for fine-tuning the way they are executed. The Break statement will break you out of the loop completely, while the Continue statement will skip the remaining part of the current loop and will go to the next iteration. These statements may be used in both "While" and "For" loops. Let's see an example of the use of continue statement for printing a string of odd numbers. In these cases, you can obtain the desired results by using the if-else statement as well, but on many occasions, the Continue statement is more convenient for expressing the idea in your mind.

```
for n in range(20):

    # if the remainder of n / 2 is 0, skip the rest of the loop

    if n % 2 == 0:

        continue

    print(n, end=' ')
```

1 3 5 7 9 11 13 15 17 19[18]

Let's see an example of the Break statement being used for less trivial tasks. The loop used here will fill up the list with the Fibonacci numbers to a particular limit:

```
a, b = 0, 1

amax = 100

L = []
```

_____

[18] *Jake VanderPlas.* Basic Python Semantics: Control flow. (2016). https://jakevdp.github.io/WhirlwindTourOfPython/07-control-flow-statements.html

```
while True:

    (a, b) = (b, a + b)

    if a > amax:

        break

    L.append(a)

print(L)
```

[1, 1, 2, 3, 5, 8, 13, 21, 34, 55, 89][19]

Note here that we have used the While True loop, which loops forever unless we have a Break statement.

Loops having an Else block

One of the most rarely used kinds of statements available in Python is the Else statement coming as a part of a "While" and a "For" loop. We have discussed the Else block before, and it executes in case the "if" and "elif" statements are evaluating to False. The Else loop is one of the most confusingly named entities in Python. One would be forced to think of the statement as a No-break statement. It means the Else block is executed just in case the loop ends naturally without coming across a Break statement.

Let's consider an example where this will be useful. Take into account this non-optimized implementation of Sieve of

---

[19] *Jake VanderPlas*. Basic Python Semantics: Control flow. (2016). https://jakevdp.github.io/WhirlwindTourOfPython/07-control-flow-statements.html

Eratosthenes, which is a well-known algorithm to find the prime numbers.

```
L = []

nmax = 30

for n in range(2, nmax):

    for factor in L:

        if n % factor == 0:

            break

    else: # no break

        L.append(n)

print(L)

[2, 3, 5, 7, 11, 13, 17, 19, 23, 29][20]
```

The Else statement will execute only when none of the factors are dividing the provided number. Here the else statement will work similar to that in the While loop.

---

[20] *Jake VanderPlas*. Basic Python Semantics: Control flow. (2016). https://jakevdp.github.io/WhirlwindTourOfPython/07-control-flow-statements.html

Expressions

Expressions refers to nothing but value representation. Expressions are different than statements in the fact that the statements will do something and expressions are the value representation. For instance, a string is an expression, and it represents the string value as well. Python comes with some advanced constructs. By using them, you will be able to represent values and therefore, these constructs are also known as expressions. In this section we will address questions like, "What are Python expressions?" and "How do I go about constructing the expressions?"

Creating the expressions

The Python expressions just contain identifiers, operators, and literals. What are they?

Identifiers: A name that is used for defining a function, class, object, or variable module is known as identifier.

Literals: They are the language independent terms of Python and need to exist independently in the programming languages. In the Python programming language you can find string literals, integer literals, floating point literals, byte literals, and imaginary literals.

Operators: By using the following operators in Python, you can implement the operations. You can use these tokens for carrying out the operations:

Operator	Token
add	+
subtract	-
multiply	*
power	**
Integer Division	/
remainder	%
decorator	@
Binary left shift	<<
Binary right shift	>>
and	&
or	\
Binary Xor	^
Binary ones complement	~
Less than	<
Greater than	>
Less than or equal to	<=
Greater than or equal to	>=
Check equality	==
Check not equal	!=

21

---

21 HackerEarth. Expressions. (2019).

Here are a few kinds of Python expressions:

List Comprehension: The List comprehension syntax is as follows -

[compute(var) for var in iterable]

For instance, the upcoming code gets you all the numbers to 10 and places them in a list.

>>> [x for x in range(10)]

[0, 1, 2, 3, 4, 5, 6, 7, 8, 9]

Dictionary Comprehension: It is practically the same as list comprehension, except that it uses curly braces.

{ k, v for k in iterable }

For instance, this upcoming code will get you all the number within 5 in the form of keys, and it will hold the corresponding squares of the numbers as values.

>>> {x:x**2 for x in range(5)}

{0: 0, 1: 1, 2: 4, 3: 9, 4: 16}

---

https://www.hackerearth.com/practice/python/working-with-data/expressions/tutorial/

Generator expression: Generator expression syntax is as shown below -

(compute(var) for var in iterable)

For instance, this following code initializes a generator object which returns values less than 10 when its object gets called.

```
>>> (x for x in range(10))
<generator object <genexpr> at 0x7fec47aee870>
>>> list(x for x in range(10))
[0, 1, 2, 3, 4, 5, 6, 7, 8, 9]
```

Conditional expressions: You may use the following constructs for the one-liner conditions.

true_value if Condition else false_value

For example:

```
>>> x = "1" if True else "2"
>>> x
'1'
```

Chapter 4: Basic Python Built-in Data Types

While we were discussing the Python objects and variables, it was stated that all the Python objects have data type info attached to them. Let's quickly go through some fundamental built-in types provided by Python. Here we are saying simple types for contrasting with many compound types that will be discussed in another section. The basic types in Python are summarized in this table:

Type	Example	Description
int	x = 1	integers (i.e., whole numbers)
float	x = 1.0	floating-point numbers (i.e., real numbers)
complex	x = 1 + 2j	Complex numbers (i.e., numbers with real and imaginary part)
bool	x = True	Boolean: True/False values
str	x = 'abc'	String: characters or text
NoneType	x = None	Special object indicating nulls[22]

---

[22] *Jake VanderPlas.* Built-In Types: Simple Values

. (2016). https://jakevdp.github.io/WhirlwindTourOfPython/05-built-in-scalar-types.html

Let's take a quick look at every one of them sequentially.

Integers: For every programming language, the fundamental type is numeric and is called an integer. All numbers that do not have decimal points are called integers.

x = 1

type(x)

Int

The Python integers are a lot more sophisticated than those found in other programming languages such as C. The C integers are precisely fixed and as a result, they overflow at a certain value such as 2^{31} or 2^{63} depending on the system. The integers in Python, on the other hand, are variable-precision. Therefore, you cannot perform computations which will overflow in other languages.

2 ** 200

1606938044258990275541962092341162602522202993782792835301376

One more useful feature of Python integer is its capability of division up-casting to the floating point by default.

5 / 2

2.5

Keep in mind that up-casting is a feature added in Python 3, while Python 2 is like other statically typed languages like C. The integer division will truncate the decimals and will return an integer.

Python 2 behavior

>>> 5 / 2

2

For recovering the same behavior in Python 3, if required, you may use floor division operators.

5 // 2

2

In the end, keep in mind that even though Python 2.x comes with both int and the long types, Python 3 can combine their behavior into one single int type.

Floating point numbers

The python floating point type is capable of storing fractional numbers. These numbers may be defined either by standard notation of decimal or in exponential notation.

x = 0.000005

y = 5e-6

print(x == y)

True

x = 1400000.00

y = 1.4e6

print(x == y)

True[23]

In your exponential notation, e or E will be read as "..times 10 to the..". Therefore 1.4e6 can be interpreted as 1.4×10^6. You can also convert an integer into a float by using the float constructor.

float(1)

1.0

Floating point precision

Keep in mind that while using the floating point arithmetic, precision level is limited. This leads to equality tests becoming unstable. For instance:

---

[23] *Jake VanderPlas*. Built-In Types: Simple Values

. (2016). https://jakevdp.github.io/WhirlwindTourOfPython/05-built-in-scalar-types.html

0.1 + 0.2 == 0.3

False

Why does this happen? As it turns out, this behavior is not unique only to Python. It happens because of the fixed precision format used by the binary floating point storage utilized by several other, if not all, of the science-based computing platforms. Every programming language that uses floating point numbers can store them in fixed bits, and it leads to some of the numbers getting presented approximately. This can be observed by printing 3 values high precision.

print("0.1 = {0:.17f}".format(0.1))

print("0.2 = {0:.17f}".format(0.2))

print("0.3 = {0:.17f}".format(0.3))

0.1 = 0.10000000000000001

0.2 = 0.20000000000000001

0.3 = 0.29999999999999999[24]

Everyone is used to thinking of numbers in a decimal notation that is to the base 10. Therefore all the fractions have to be

---

[24] *Jake VanderPlas*. Built-In Types: Simple Values

. (2016). https://jakevdp.github.io/WhirlwindTourOfPython/05-built-in-scalar-types.html

expressed as the addition of powers of ten.

$$1/8 = 1.10^{-1} + 2.10^{-2} + 5.10^{-3}$$

In a base 10 representation that we are accustomed to, we will represent the output in a familiar expression, which is 0.125. The computers normally store values in binary notations. Therefore, every number is expressed as the addition of powers of two.

$$1/8 = 0.2^{-1} + 0.2^{-2} + 1.2^{-3}$$

In the "to the base 2" representation you may write this as $[0.001]\_2$ and the subscript here indicates the binary notation. Here the value of $0.125 = [0.001]\_2$ is one number that can be represented by both decimal and binary notations and gets represented by a finite number of digits. In the familiar "to the base 10" representation of numbers, there are some numbers that cannot be expressed as a finite number of digits. For instance, dividing 1 by 3 will give, in standard decimal notation:

$$1/3 = 0.333333333\ldots$$

Here the 3s will go on infinitely. It means that for representing the quotient, the required number of digits is infinite. Much in the same manner, you will have numbers for whom binary representation needs an infinite number of digits. For instance:

1/10 = ⟦0.0.00011001100110011...⟧ _2

Similar to a decimal notation which requires an infinite number of digits for representing 1/3 perfectly, the binary notation needs an infinite number of digits for representing 1/10. The programming language will truncate the representation at the level of 52 bits at most after the first non-zero bit in the case of most systems. The rounding error for the floating point value is a necessary problem for working with the floating point numbers. One of the easiest ways of dealing with this is by keeping in mind that the floating point arithmetic will be approximate and will not rely on precise equality tests having floating point values.

Complex numbers

Numbers having real and imaginary parts (also called floating points) are complex numbers. We have already checked real numbers and integers. These two can be used for constructing complex numbers.

complex(1, 2)

(1+2j)

Otherwise, we can use the suffix "j" present in equations for indicating the imaginary parts.

1 + 2j

(1+2j)

The complex numbers come with a range of interesting methods and attributes. These can be seen in the examples below.

c = 3 + 4j

c.real # real part

3.0

c.imag # imaginary part

4.0

c.conjugate() # complex conjugate

(3-4j)

abs(c) # magnitude, i.e. sqrt(c.real ** 2 + c.imag ** 2)

5.0 [25]

String Type

Python strings are created by using single or double quotes.

message = "what do you like?"

response = 'spam'

There are many useful methods and string functions available in Python. Here are some of them:

---

[25] *Jake VanderPlas.* Built-In Types: Simple Values

. (2016). https://jakevdp.github.io/WhirlwindTourOfPython/05-built-in-scalar-types.html

```
# length of string
len(response)
4
# Make upper-case. See also str.lower()
response.upper()
'SPAM'
# Capitalize. See also str.title()
message.capitalize()
'What do you like?'
# concatenation with +
message + response
'what do you like?spam'
# multiplication is multiple concatenation
5 * response
'spamspamspamspamspam'
# Access individual characters (zero-based indexing)
message[0]
'w'
```
[26]

---

[26] *Jake VanderPlas*. Built-In Types: Simple Values

. (2016). https://jakevdp.github.io/WhirlwindTourOfPython/05-built-in-

None Type

There is a special type available in Python and it is None type. It has only one single value possible and that is None. For instance:

type(None)

NoneType

You will find None used in several places, however, the most commonly used one is a function's default return value. For instance, the print function of Python in Python 3 will not return anything. However we can yet catch the value:

return_value = print('abc')

abc

print(return_value)

None

Similarly, other functions in Python having no return value are in reality returning None.

Boolean Type

Boolean type in Python is a relatively straightforward type with just 2 possible values - True and False. The type is returned by using comparison operators which were discussed prior to this.

result = (4 < 5)

result

---

scalar-types.html

True

type(result)

Bool

Remember that the Boolean values are case sensitive and dissimilar to other programming languages. The "True" and "False" have to be capitalized.

print(True, False)

True False

Booleans may also be constructed by using bool() object constructor. The values of other types may also be turned into Boolean through some predictable rules. For instance, all numeric types are false if they equal to zero and are otherwise True.

bool(2014)

True

bool(0)

False

bool(3.1415)

True

Boolean conversion in the None type is typically False.

bool(None)

False

For the strings bool(s) will be False for empty strings and otherwise it will be True.

bool("")

False

bool("abc")

True

For the sequences that we are going to see later Boolean representation will be False in case of empty sequences and it will be True for other kinds of sequences.

bool([1, 2, 3])

True

bool([])

False

Chapter 5: Setting up Python: Installation and Setup

For beginning your work on Python 3, you must have access to the Python interpreters. There are many ways of accomplishing this. The programming language can be obtained from the Python software foundation site (python.org). This normally involves downloading the necessary installers specific to your operating system and then running the software on your computer. Some of the OSs will provide a package manager, notably Linux, which should be run for installing Python. If you have Mac as your OS, the best way of installing Python 3 is by installing the package manager Homebrew. How to do this is described later in this chapter. If you are using a cell phone operating systems such as iOS or Android, you may install apps which supply you with the Python programming environment. It is a great way to practice your coding capabilities on the go. Apart from this, you will find many sites online which allow you to access Python interpreter online without having to install anything on your machine at all. It is also a possibility that Python is shipped along with your operating system purchase and is installed already. Although that might be the case, there is a possibility that the Python installed version is outdated, and in such a case you will wish to get the latest version. In this chapter, we will see how to install Python step-by-step to set up Python 3 distribution on Mac OS, Linux, Windows, iOS, and Android. Without further ado, let's get started.

Windows

Although it is possible that your Windows computer is shipped with Python already installed, it is unlikely. Most Windows systems do not ship with Python installed on them. Luckily, installing Python on Windows is not much trouble. All you need to do is download the installer from your python.org site and run it. Let's take a closer look at installing Python 3 for Windows.

Step 1: Downloading the installer for Python 3:

Open your browser window and go to the "Download" page for Windows available at python.org. Under that heading at the top it will say, "Python Releases for Windows." Click on the "Latest Python 3 Release-Python 3.x.x." When this book was written, the latest version of Python was 3.6.5. Now, scroll to the bottom and select either Windows x86-64 executable installer or Windows x86 executable installer[27], for 64 and 32 bit respectively.

Now the question is - which is better? The 32 bit or 64 bit Python? If you consider Windows, you may choose either installer. Here are the differences between the two: If your computer has a 32-bit processor, you might wish to select the 32-bit installer. If you have a 64-bit system, you may use either of the installers for most uses. The 32-bit version uses up less memory. However, the 64 bit performs better for the applications having intensive computation. If you are unsure what version to go with, select the 64-bit version.

---

[27] Real Python. Python 3 Installation & Setup Guide. (2018). https://realpython.com/installing-python/

Keep in mind that if you get the selection wrong and would prefer to ship to another Python version, all you need to do is uninstall Python and again re-install by downloading the suitable installer from python.org.

Step 2: Running the installer: When you have selected and downloaded the installer of your choice, just run it by double clicking on the downloaded file. You will find a dialog opening which will look like this:

Remember here to be sure to check the box which says "Add Python 3.x to PATH" as displayed here to make sure that the interpreters are placed in the execution path. After this, click on Install Now. This is all that is required. Sometime later, you will have a working version of Python 3 installed on the system.

---

28 Real Python. Python 3 Installation & Setup Guide. (2018). https://realpython.com/installing-python/

WSL (Windows Subsystem for Linux)

If you are running Windows 10 the Creators of Anniversary update on your computer, you will, in reality, have another option to install Python. The versions of Windows 10 which include this feature called WSL will allow you to run the Linux environment directly on Windows unmodified without having the virtual machine overhead.

You can find more information about WSL on the Microsoft official website. For instructions regarding enabling the subsystems in Windows 10 and installing Linux distribution, check out the Windows 10 installation guide available online. You may also want to check out the presentation available on YouTube made by one of the members of WSL development team.

Linux

It is quite possible that your Linux distribution will have Python installed already. But it is also possible that this is not the latest version of Python. It is likely to be Python 2 rather than Python 3. In order to find out which version of Python you have installed, you can open a terminal window and use these upcoming commands:

python --version

python2 --version

python3 --version

One of these commands will respond telling you the version like this:

$ python3 --version

Python 3.6.5

If it displays the version to be Python 2.x.x or some other version of Python 3 which isn't the latest version, then you might wish to install the latest Python version. The procedure involved in doing this depends mainly on the Linux distribution you are running on your computer. Keep in mind here that it is simpler to use a tool called pynev for managing multiple Python versions on this OS. You can find more information about it online.

Ubuntu

The Python installation instructions will vary depending on the Ubuntu distribution version you are running on your machine. It is possible to find out the local Ubuntu version by running this command:

$ lsb_release -a

No LSB modules are available.

Distributor ID: Ubuntu

Description: Ubuntu 16.04.4 LTS

Release: 16.04

Codename: xenial[29]

What you can see under "Release" in your console output is the version number of Ubuntu. Now follow these instructions below:

---

[29] Real Python. Python 3 Installation & Setup Guide. (2018). https://realpython.com/installing-python/

Ubuntu 17.10, Ubuntu 18.04 and above will be available with Python 3.6. It is possible to invoke Python by using the command python3. However, Ubuntu 16.10 and 17.04 do not have Python 3.6 by default. It is available in their Universe repository. It is possible to install it by using these commands:

$ sudo apt-get update

$ sudo apt-get install python3.6

You may invoke it by using the command python3.6. But, if you are using Ubuntu 14.04 or 16.04, you will not find Python 3.6 in their Universe repository. You are required to get it from the Personal Package Archive. For instance, for installing Python from the PPA deadsnakes, you can follow these steps:

$ sudo add-apt-repository ppa:deadsnakes/ppa

$ sudo apt-get update

$ sudo apt-get install python3.6[30]

Similar to the description above, this will invoke Python with the command python3.6.

Linux Mint

Both Ubuntu and Linux use the exact same package management system, and it often makes your life easier. You

---

[30] Real Python. Python 3 Installation & Setup Guide. (2018). https://realpython.com/installing-python/

may follow the steps provided for Ubuntu 14.04 for this purpose. The PPA deadsnakes will work with Mint.

Debian

There are resources available online that suggest that the method used for Ubuntu 16.10 will also work for Debian. However, there was no specific path to get it to work on this OS (Debian 9). If you try, you will probably end up getting Python from the resources listed below. There is one problem with Debian, though. It does not by default install the sudo command. For installing it, you will have to do this even before carrying out the instructions for compiling python from a source like these:

$ su

$ apt-get install sudo

$ vi /etc/sudoers

After completing this, open the /etc/sudoers file by using the sudo vim command, or you may use your text editor for the purpose. Incorporate the following line of text at the file end and replace your_username with the real username.

your_username ALL=(ALL) ALL

openSUSE

There are many websites on internet that describe how to get the zypper installing the latest Python version. However, they appeared troublesome or plain outdated. It was not possible to get any of them to work seamlessly, so it will be a better idea to build Python from source. To do this you will have to install development tools. This can be done in the YaST by using the menus or with the zypper.

$ sudu zypper install -t pattern devel_C_C++

Implementing the step takes a while and it involves installing 154 packages. However, when it is completed, it becomes probable to build the resource like shown in the Compiling Python from Source section.

CentOS

We have the IUS community that provides newer versions of software to the Enterprise Linux distros that is Red Hat Enterprise and CentOS. It is possible to use this work for helping you install Python 3. To install Python, you need to update the system first by using the yum package manager.

$ sudo yum update

$ sudo yum install yum-utils

The CentOS |US package can be installed after this and will allow you to become up-to-date with their website.

$ sudo yum install https://centos7.iuscommunity.org/ius-release.rpm

And now lastly you may install Python and Pip.

$ sudo yum install python36u

$ sudo yum install python36u-pip

Fedora

Fedora comes with a roadmap for switching to Python 3 by default. It is published online. The roadmap indicates that their latest version and the versions coming up will be shipped with Python 2 by default, however, Python 3 will get installed. In case Python 3 is installed on your Fedora version and it is not 3.6 version, you might make use of this command for installing it:

$ sudo dnf install python36

Arch Linux

This OS is pretty aggressive with being up-to-date with the Python releases. It is possible that you may already possess its latest version. If you don't, use this command to get it:

$ packman -S python

Compile Python from the source

The Linux distribution might not come with the latest Python version at times. Or you might wish to build the greatest and latest version by yourself. So, let's look at the steps involved in building Python from its source.

Step 1: Downloading the source code: In the beginning, you need to get a hold of Python source code. This is fairly easy to obtain from python.org. If you go to the Download page, you will find the latest Python 3 source at the top of the page. Ensure that you do not get the legacy Python (Python 2). After you have selected the right version, you can find a Files section at the bottom end of the page. Choose the Gzipped source tarball for downloading the version to your computer. In the event you like the command line method, you may use wget for downloading to the current directory easily.

$ wget https://www.python.org/ftp/python/3.6.5/Python-3.6.5.tgz

Step 2: Preparing the system: You will find that there are some distro-specific steps necessary for building Python from nothing. Its target is the same as all the distros. However, you may be required to translate to the distribution in the event it doesn't use apt-get.

1. The very first step for performing an operation like this is updating the system packages on your computer before beginning. In the case of Debian, this is how it should look:

$ sudo apt-get update

$ sudo apt-get upgrade

2. The next step is to ensure that the system comes with all the necessary tools for building Python. You will require quite a few of them, but you might possess some of them already and that is fine. You can find them all listed here in a single command line. However, you may break the list in shorter commands just with the repetition of sudo apt-get install -y portion.

For apt-based systems (like Debian, Ubuntu, and Mint)

$ sudo apt-get install -y make build-essential libssl-dev zlib1g-dev libbz2-dev libreadline-dev libsqlite3-dev wget curl llvm libncurses5-dev libncursesw5-dev xz-utils tk-dev

For yum-based systems (like CentOS)

$ sudo yum -y groupinstall development

$ sudo yum -y install zlib-devel[31]

---

[31] Real Python. Python 3 Installation & Setup Guide. (2018).

Step 3: Building Python:

1. When you have all the prerequisites along with the tar file, the next step is to unpack your resource in a directory. Make a note here that the upcoming command can create a new directory, which is called Python 3.6.5 and is under the directory you are in.

$ tar xvf Python-3.6.5.tgz

$ cd Python-3.6.5

2. After this, you will be required to run your ./configure tool for preparing the build.

$ ./configure --enable-optimizations --with-ensurepip=install

3. After this, you will build Python programs by using the make. You will find that the -j option merely tells the make to split the program building into parallel steps for speeding up the compilation process. Even in case of parallel builds the step can take a few minutes.

$ make -j 8

4. After this, install the newer version of Python. The altinstall target is used here to ensure that there is no overwriting of the Python system version. As you are installing Python in /usr/bin, you are required to run as root:

$ sudo make altinstall

---

https://realpython.com/installing-python/

Make a note here that you must only use the altinstall target for the make. If you use the install target, it will overwrite the Python binary. There are many sections of the system which rely on Python's pre-installed version.

Step 4: Verifying the Python install: Lastly, you may test the new Python version you have installed.

$ python3.6 -V

Python 3.6.5

macOS or macOS X

You can find Python 2 on the current version of the Mac operating system called macOS. It was also known as Mac OS X previously. However, it is likely to be out of date by some months. We are using the code used in Python 3. After some research, it was decided that the best way of installing Python 3 on macOS is by using the Homebrew package manager. The method is recommended by the community guides of Python such as Hitchhiker's guide as well.

Step 1: Installing Homebrew Part one: Before getting started, you may wish to install the Homebrew.

1: Open the browser and go to http://brew.sh/. When the page has loaded, opt for the Homebrew bootstrap code which can be found under "Install Homebrew". After this press Cmd + C for copying it to your clipboard. Ensure that here you have collected the text for the complete command as otherwise, the installation may fail.

2. After this, you must open a terminal.app window and paste that Homebrew bootstrap code there. Now, press the Enter button. All of this will lead to the beginning of the Homebrew installation.

3. In case you are doing this on the fresh installing of macOS, there is a likelihood of getting a pop-up alert which will ask you to install Apple "command line developer tools." These will be required for continuation of installation. Therefore, now confirm to the dialogue box with the clicking of "Install."

At this juncture, you will be waiting for the installation of command line developer tools and it takes a few minutes.

Step 2: Installing Homebrew Part 2:

You may continue the installation of Homebrew and later Python after the installation of command line developer tools is complete. When the dialog "The software was installed" appears, confirm it from your developer tools installer. Get back to the terminal and hit Enter for the continuation of Homebrew installation. Homebrew will ask you to enter the password, as it can finalize the installation after that. Here, enter the user account passcode and press Enter for continuation. Homebrew will take a few minutes depending on the internet connection to download the necessary files. When the installation is finished you will be back to the command prompt present in the terminal window. This means that the setting up of the package manager is complete. Now we go for the installation of Python 3 on your computer.

Step 3: Installing Python

When you have finished installing Homebrew, go back to the terminal and run this command:

$ brew install python3

Keep in mind that once you copy the command, you are not including the $ character at the start. It is only an indicator that this was a console command. It will download and install the Python latest version on your machine. After completing the Homebrew install command, you will have Python 3 installed on the computer. You may also ensure that everything went off smoothly by testing whether Python may be accessed from the machine.

You can open the terminal with the launching of Terminal.app. Then type pip3 and enter. The Pip package manager of Python will show you its help text. In case you have an error message while running the pip3, go to the Python installing steps again to make sure that you have a proper working installation of Python.

Now, assuming that things went on well and you are able to see the output from Pip on the command prompt window, it means you have successfully installed Python on the machine and you are all ready for continuation to the next section.

iOS used for iPhone and iPad

There is a full-fledged development environment from Python for iOS and it is called Pythonista app. It can run on any iPhone or iPad. It is fundamentally a blend of a Python editor, interpreter, and documentation all rolled into one single app. Pythonista is surprisingly enjoyable to use. It comes with a fantastic tool which can be used when you are stuck without your computer and wish to work on Python. It has a full Python 3 standard library and also has the full documentation which is otherwise available online. For installing and setting up Pythonista, you are required to download it from an app store catering to iOS.

Android Tablets and Phones

If you have any of the Android tablets or phones and wish to use or practice Python on them while on the go, you will find several options for doing so. The one option that can be used reliably and supports Python 3.6 is Pydroid 3. It comes with an interpreter that can be used for the REPL sessions and it gives the capability to save, edit, and execute the Python code as well.

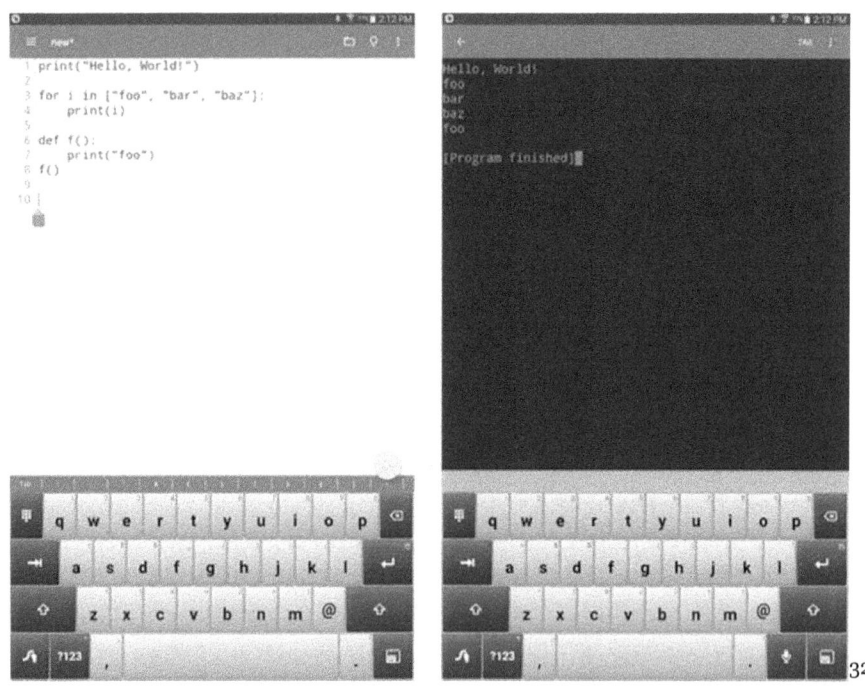

Pydroid3 can be downloaded and installed from the Google Play Store. You can find a free and a paid premium version there which will support code predictions along with the code analysis.

Python interpreters online

---

32 Real Python. Python 3 Installation & Setup Guide. (2018). https://realpython.com/installing-python/

If you are looking to try out various examples without having to install Python on your computer, you will find many sites where it is possible to interact with Python interpreters online. Some of the examples are python.org online console, Python Fiddle, Repl.it, Python Anywhere, and Trinket. These are cloud-based interpreters for Python and they may not be able to execute the more complex sample examples. However, they are adequate to run the simple ones, and this is a nice way of getting you started. You can find more info about using these websites online.

This chapter covered all the information needed for gaining access to the Python 3 interpreters.

Chapter 6: Data Structures in Python

Data structures are exactly what their name suggests - structures. They can hold the data in one place. In other words, the data structures are used for storing a collection of relative data. You can find 4 built-in data structures for Python. They are lists, tuple, set, and dictionary. In this section, we will see how to use every one of them and learn how they make things easier for us.

List

The first data structure is the list. It holds a sequenced collection of items that you may store sequentially in the list. It is easy to imagine by thinking of shopping lists, where you possess a list of items to buy, except that every item may be on a separate line on the physical list. In Python, you will place commas between them. This list of items must be enclosed in square braces in order for Python to understand that a list is being specified. When the list is created you may add, remove, or search the items from that list. As it is possible to add or remove items from the list, we are able to say that the list is a mutable data type, meaning it can be altered.

An introduction to objects and classes

A brief discussion on objects and classes is needed here to understand the lists better. The list is an example of the use of classes and objects. If we have used a variable called "i" and assigned some value to it, say 5, it is called as creating an object or an instance. In other words, "i" of the class int. You might want to read help(int) for understanding this concept better.

A class will also have methods, that is, some functions which are defined for use in respect to that specific class. You may use these functionality pieces only at the time when you possess the object of a class. For instance, Python gives you one append method for your list class, and it allows you to add an entity to the end of a list. For instance, mylist.apend('an item') will add the specific string to your list called mylist. Note here the dotted notation for accessing object methods.

Your class may also have fields that happen to be nothing but variables which are defined for use in respect to the class. These variables or names can be used only when you own the object of a class. Fields also get accessed via the dotted notation. For instance, mylist.field. E.g. save as ds_using_list.py.

```python
# This is my shopping list

shoplist = ['apple', 'mango', 'carrot', 'banana']


print('I have', len(shoplist), 'items to purchase.')


print('These items are:', end=' ')

for item in shoplist:

    print(item, end=' ')
```

```
print('\nI also have to buy rice.')

shoplist.append('rice')

print('My shopping list is now', shoplist)


print('I will sort my list now')

shoplist.sort()

print('Sorted shopping list is', shoplist)


print('The first item I will buy is', shoplist[0])

olditem = shoplist[0]

del shoplist[0]

print('I bought the', olditem)

print('My shopping list is now', shoplist)
```
[33]

It's output is:

```
$ python ds_using_list.py
I have 4 items to purchase.
These items are: apple mango carrot banana
I also have to buy rice.
```

---

[33] Data Structures. https://python.swaroopch.com/data_structures.html

My shopping list is now ['apple', 'mango', 'carrot', 'banana', 'rice']

I will sort my list now

Sorted shopping list is ['apple', 'banana', 'carrot', 'mango', 'rice']

The first item I will buy is apple

I bought the apple

My shopping list is now ['banana', 'carrot', 'mango', 'rice'][34]

How does it work?

Your shoplist variable is one shopping list for a person going to the market. In this variable, we can just store name strings of the different items to purchase. However, you may add any different object to this list including numbers and their lists. Here a for..in loop has also been used to iterate through various items on the list. You may have realized by now that the lists are also sequences and the specialty of the sequences is discussed elsewhere. Note here that the use of end parameter while calling the print functions will indicate that we are looking to end the output with spacing rather than using a line break.

Now we will add an item to this list by utilizing the append method of your list object as described earlier. After this, we can check whether the item has been added to the list or not by printing the contents of this list by passing this list to the function print, and it will print the list correctly. Now we will sort out the list by utilizing the sort method in the list. It is significant here that you understand that the method will affect

---

[34] Data Structures. https://python.swaroopch.com/data_structures.html

the list and will not return a modified list. It is not similar to how the strings work. It is what is meant when it is said that lists are mutable and conversely the strings are not (or are immutable).

Now, when we finish the purchase of some item from the market, we may wish to remove it from the original list. This can be done by using the del statement. Here we will mention what item of the list we wish to remove and the del statement will do this needful for you. You may want to specify here that you wish to remove the first item from the list, so we make use of del shoplist[0]. Keep in mind here that Python begins counting from zero. If you want to find out all methods defined by this list object, go to the help(list) for more details.

Tuple

A tuple is utilized for holding together several objects. They are similar to the lists but do not have the extensive functionality which is provided by the list class. One of the significant features of tuples is that they happen to be immutable, much like the strings. It means that you can modify them. They are defined by specification of items that are separated with commas enclosed in an optional pair of braces. They are extensively used in the cases where user defined functions or statements are in a position to assume that the collected values will not change. In other words the tuple of values utilized will not change.

For instance, save as ds_using_tuple.py

```
# I would recommend always using parentheses

# to indicate start and end of tuple

# even though parentheses are optional.

# Explicit is better than implicit.

zoo = ('python', 'elephant', 'penguin')

print('Number of animals in the zoo is', len(zoo))

new_zoo = 'monkey', 'camel', zoo    # parentheses not required
but are a good idea

print('Number of cages in the new zoo is', len(new_zoo))

print('All animals in new zoo are', new_zoo)

print('Animals brought from old zoo are', new_zoo[2])

print('Last animal brought from old zoo is', new_zoo[2][2])

print('Number of animals in the new zoo is',

    len(new_zoo)-1+len(new_zoo[2]))
```
[35]

Its output is:

```
$ python ds_using_tuple.py

Number of animals in the zoo is 3

Number of cages in the new zoo is 3
```

---

[35] Data Structures. https://python.swaroopch.com/data_structures.html

All animals in new zoo are ('monkey', 'camel', ('python', 'elephant', 'penguin'))

Animals brought from old zoo are ('python', 'elephant', 'penguin')

Last animal brought from old zoo is penguin

Number of animals in the new zoo is 5[36]

How does it work?

Your variable zoo indicates a tuple of items. Here we can observe that the "len" function may be utilized in order to have the tuple length. It also refers to the fact that the tuple is a sequence. Now, we will shift the animals to a new zoo due to the fact that the old zoo will be closed. Therefore the new_zoo tuple will contain many animals that are already there together with the animals which were brought there from the old zoo. Coming back to reality, keep in mind that a tuple inside a tuple doesn't lose its identity.

The items in the tuple may be accessed by specifying the position of the item in a pair of square braces similar to what we did while doing the lists. It is called an indexing operator. The third term in the new_zoo can be accessed by mentioning new_zoo[2] and the 3rd item inside the 3rd item of new_zoo tuple will be accessed by specifying new_zoo[2][2]. If you have understood this idiom, it is pretty straightforward.

A tuple having 0 or 1 items: Any empty tuple gets constructed with the empty pair of braces like myempty = (). But a tuple having a single item will not be so straightforward. You must specify it clearly by using commas following the 1st

---

[36] Data Structures. https://python.swaroopch.com/data_structures.html

and the only item. This is because Python may be able to differentiate between a pair of braces around an object and a tuple in one expression. That is, you must specify singleton = (2,) in case you wish to say that you want a tuple having an item 2.

A reminder for Perl Programmers: If you have a list inside a list, the original one will not lose its identity. It means that the lists are not flattened like in the case of Perl. The very same thing applies to the tuples within a tuple. Or for a tuple inside a list or a list inside a tuple and so on. And as far as Python is concerned, these are all just objects that are stored by using other objects, and that's it.

Dictionary

The dictionary is similar to an address book in which you can find different addresses and contact details of people by knowing their names. That is, in this case, we are associating the keys (names) to the values (details). Make a note here that the keys have to be unique similar to a situation where there are two persons having the same name and as a result, you are not able to locate the correct information corresponding to them. Keep in mind here that you may only use immutable objects here for the keys (such as strings) of your dictionary. However, you may use either mutable or immutable objects for your values in the dictionary. It fundamentally means that you should be using only the simple object for your keys.

The key pairs and values are specified inside a dictionary by using notations d = {key1 : value1, key2 : value 2}. Note here that the two key-value pairs are being separated by a colon and the pairs are separated with commas, and everything is encompassed within a pair of parentheses. Keep in mind that the key-value pairs inside a dictionary will not be ordered in any particular manner. In case you wish for a specific order, you must be able to sort them out before actually using them.

The actual dictionaries you use are in reality objects or instances of the dict class. For instance, save as ds_using_dict.py.

```python
# 'ab' is short for 'a'ddress'b'ook

ab = {
    'Swaroop': 'swaroop@swaroopch.com',

    'Larry': 'larry@wall.org',

    'Matsumoto': 'matz@ruby-lang.org',

    'Spammer': 'spammer@hotmail.com'
}
print("Swaroop's address is", ab['Swaroop'])

# Deleting a key-value pair

del ab['Spammer']

print('\nThere are {} contacts in the address-book\n'.format(len(ab)))

for name, address in ab.items():

    print('Contact {} at {}'.format(name, address))

# Adding a key-value pair
```

ab['Guido'] = 'guido@python.org'

if 'Guido' in ab:

print("\nGuido's address is", ab['Guido'])

And its output is:

$ python ds_using_dict.py

Swaroop's address is swaroop@swaroopch.com

There are 3 contacts in the address-book

Contact Swaroop at swaroop@swaroopch.com

Contact Matsumoto at matz@ruby-lang.org

Contact Larry at larry@wall.org

Guido's address is guido@python.org[37]

How does it work?

We have created a dictionary ab by using the notations discussed earlier. Now we can access the key-value pairs with a specification of keys by using indexing operators discussed earlier in the context of tuples and lists. Note the easy syntax here. It is also possible to delete the key-value pairs by using your old friend "del" statement. Here, only specify the dictionary and indexing operator for your key to be removed and passed on to this "del" statement. It is not mandatory to

---

[37] Data Structures. https://python.swaroopch.com/data_structures.html

know the value that corresponds to your key for the operation.

After this, we will access every key-value pair of your dictionary by using items method in the dictionary which will return a tuples' list, in which each tuple has a pair of items in the form, key followed by a value. We can retrieve the pair and assign it to variables name and address that correspond to every pair that uses the for...in loop, and then print these values in the "for" block of the code. Newer key-value pairs could be added just by utilizing the indexing operator for accessing the key and assigning the value, as done for the Guido in the case above. We may verify here whether the key-value pair exists by using the "in" operator. For getting the list of methods for the dict class check out help(dict).

Dictionaries and Keyword arguments: If you have utilized keyword arguments inside the functions, it means you have already used the dictionaries. Just give it a thought. Key-value pair gets specified by you in your list of parameters of the function definition. Now, when you access the variables inside the function, it will be only key access of the dictionary and it is called symbol table in the terminology used for compiler design.

Sequence

Strings, lists and tuples are all examples of sequences. Let's now see what sequences are and why they are so special. Major features of sequences are membership tests i.e. in and not in expressions and the indexing operations that empower us to fetch specific items in a sequence directly. There are 3 types of sequences mentioned above viz, strings, lists, and tuples. They also possess a slicing operation that permits us to retrieve a portion (slice) of the sequence, meaning a part of the sequence. For example, save as ds_seq.py.

```python
shoplist = ['apple', 'mango', 'carrot', 'banana']

name = 'swaroop'

# Indexing or 'Subscription' operation #

print('Item 0 is', shoplist[0])

print('Item 1 is', shoplist[1])

print('Item 2 is', shoplist[2])

print('Item 3 is', shoplist[3])

print('Item -1 is', shoplist[-1])

print('Item -2 is', shoplist[-2])

print('Character 0 is', name[0])

# Slicing on a list #

print('Item 1 to 3 is', shoplist[1:3])

print('Item 2 to end is', shoplist[2:])

print('Item 1 to -1 is', shoplist[1:-1])

print('Item start to end is', shoplist[:])

# Slicing on a string #

print('characters 1 to 3 is', name[1:3])

print('characters 2 to end is', name[2:])
```

print('characters 1 to -1 is', name[1:-1])

print('characters start to end is', name[:])[38]

Its output is:

$ python ds_seq.py

Item 0 is apple

Item 1 is mango

Item 2 is carrot

Item 3 is banana

Item -1 is banana

Item -2 is carrot

Character 0 is s

Item 1 to 3 is ['mango', 'carrot']

Item 2 to end is ['carrot', 'banana']

Item 1 to -1 is ['mango', 'carrot']

Item start to end is ['apple', 'mango', 'carrot', 'banana']

characters 1 to 3 is wa

characters 2 to end is aroop

---

[38] Data Structures. https://python.swaroopch.com/data_structures.html

characters 1 to -1 is waroo

characters start to end is swaroop[39]

How does it work?

Initially, we will see how to use indexes for getting individual items of sequences. It is also referred to as subscription operations. Once you have specified the sequence number inside square braces as displayed above, Python can fetch the item for you which is corresponding to the sequence position. Keep in mind that Python begins counting numbers from 0. Therefore, shoplist [0] will fetch the 1st item and the shoplist [3] will get 4th from the shoplist sequence. This index may also be a -ve number and in that case, the position gets calculated from the sequence end. So, shoplist [-1] will refer to the last item of the sequence.

Slicing items are used by mentioning the names of the sequences which is followed by the optional number pairs separated by a colon inside square braces. Make a note here that it is similar to indexing operations you were using thus far. Also, keep it in mind that the numbers are optional and the colon isn't.

The initial number before the colon during the slicing operation will refer to a position from where slicing starts, and the 2nd number coming after the colon will indicate where the slice can stop. If the 1st number is not given, Python will use the beginning of the sequence as the starting point. If the 2nd number is to be left out, Python stops near the end of the sequence. Notice here that slice has returned "starts" at the starting position and it will end near the "end" position. This

---

[39] Data Structures. https://python.swaroopch.com/data_structures.html

means the start position is included, however the end position is not in the sequence slice.

Therefore, shoplist [1:3} will return a slice of your sequence beginning position 1 and include position 2 and will stop at position 3. So, a slice of 2 items will be returned. In the same manner, shoplist [:] will return a copy of the total sequence. It is also possible to perform slicing in negative positions. The negative numbers are utilized for various positions starting from the end of the sequence. For instance, shoplist [:-1] returns a sequence slice that excludes the sequence's last item but at the same time contains everything else. One can also give the slice a 3rd argument which is called "step" for slicing. The step size is 1 by default.

```
>>> shoplist = ['apple', 'mango', 'carrot', 'banana']

>>> shoplist[::1]

['apple', 'mango', 'carrot', 'banana']

>>> shoplist[::2]

['apple', 'carrot']

>>> shoplist[::3]

['apple', 'banana']

>>> shoplist[::-1]

['banana', 'carrot', 'mango', 'apple']
```[40]

---

[40] Data Structures. https://python.swaroopch.com/data_structures.html

Note here in step 2, we will get items having position 0, 2. Once the step size gets to 3 we will get items having positions 0, 3, etc. You may try different combinations of these kinds of slice specifications by using Python interpreter interactively, as you will be able to see the results quickly. A great thing about the sequences is that it is possible to access lists, strings, and tuples all in the same manner.

Set

A set is an unordered collection of simple objects. Sets are utilized when the object existence in a collection is more significant than the order in which they appear or the number of times they occur. You may test for membership by using the sets. Whether it happens to be a subset or a different set altogether, look for the intersection between 2 sets and so forth.

```
>>> bri = set(['brazil', 'russia', 'india'])

>>> 'india' in bri

True

>>> 'usa' in bri

False

>>> bric = bri.copy()

>>> bric.add('china')

>>> bric.issuperset(bri)
```

True

>>> bri.remove('russia')

>>> bri & bric # OR bri.intersection(bric)

{'brazil', 'india'}[41]

How does it work?

If you remember the basic set theory you must have learned in mathematics while in school, then the example is pretty much self-explanatory. However, if you have not learned it, Google for set theory and also for Venn diagram to better understand the use of sets in Python.

References

Once you have created an object and assigned it to a variable, then the variable just refers to the object and will not represent the object actually. It means that the variable name will point to a part of your computer memory where the object gets stored. It is known as binding the name to the object. Normally, there is no need to worry about it, however, you will find a subtle effect because of the references you need to be conscious of. For instance, save as ds_reference.py.

print('Simple Assignment')

shoplist = ['apple', 'mango', 'carrot', 'banana']

---

[41] Data Structures. https://python.swaroopch.com/data_structures.html

```
# mylist is just another name pointing to the same object!

mylist = shoplist

# I purchased the first item, so I remove it from the list

del shoplist[0]

print('shoplist is', shoplist)

print('mylist is', mylist)

# Notice that both shoplist and mylist both print

# the same list without the 'apple' confirming that

# they point to the same object

print('Copy by making a full slice')

# Make a copy by doing a full slice

mylist = shoplist[:]

# Remove first item

del mylist[0]

print('shoplist is', shoplist)

print('mylist is', mylist)
```
[42]

```
# Notice that now the two lists are different
```

---

[42] Data Structures. https://python.swaroopch.com/data_structures.html

Its output is:

$ python ds_reference.py

Simple Assignment

shoplist is ['mango', 'carrot', 'banana']

mylist is ['mango', 'carrot', 'banana']

Copy by making a full slice

shoplist is ['mango', 'carrot', 'banana']

mylist is ['carrot', 'banana'][43]

How does it work?

Most of the explanation can be found in the comments. Keep in mind that in case you are looking to create a copy of lists or similar kind of sequences or complicated objects (not the easy objects like integers), then you will be required to use slicing operators for making a copy. If you are assigning the variable name to a name, they will both refer to the same object. This can be the trouble if you are not careful.

One note for the Perl programmers here - keep in mind that the assignment statements for your list do not create copies. You need to use slicing operators for making copies of the sequence.

Some facts about strings

Although we have understood what strings are, there are certain things you may wish to know about them. Are you aware that the strings also happen to be objects and contain

---

[43] Data Structures. https://python.swaroopch.com/data_structures.html

methods that do everything from verifying a part of a string to stripping spaces? As a matter of fact, you have already seen the use of a string method in the form of format method.

The different strings you make use of in the programs are objects of the class str*. In the upcoming example, we can see some useful methods of the class. For a full list of these methods, check out help(str). For example, save as ds_str_methods.py.

```python
# This is a string object
name = 'Swaroop'
if name.startswith('Swa'):
    print('Yes, the string starts with "Swa"')
if 'a' in the name:
    print('Yes, it contains the string "a"')
if name.find('war') != -1:
    print('Yes, it contains the string "war"')
delimiter = '_*_'
mylist = ['Brazil', 'Russia', 'India', 'China']
print(delimiter.join(mylist))
```

Its output is:

```
$ python ds_str_methods.py
Yes, the string starts with "Swa"
```

Yes, it contains the string "a"

Yes, it contains the string "war"

Brazil_*_Russia_*_India_*_China

How does it work?

In this case, we can see many string methods in use. The starts with the method are utilized for finding out if the string starts with a provided string. Here the in operator is utilized for checking out if the provided string is part of the string. Here the find method is utilized for locating the position of given substrings within a string. The find will return -1 if it is not successful in finding substrings. You can find the "str" class a neat method as well to "join" these items of the sequence with the provided string working as a delimiter between every item of sequence and then return the bigger generated strings.

Summary

Here we have seen different built-in data structures of Python. They are necessary for writing programs of a certain size. Now that many Python basics are in place, we can now write the real world programs in Python.

Chapter 7: Web Development Using Django

Django was invented and developed to cater to the fast-moving deadlines of newsrooms, and at the same time satisfy the difficult requirements of experienced web developers. By using Django, you can move the web applications from concept to launch within a matter of a few hours. Django will take care of all the hassle during web development so that you are able to focus on writing code for the app without having to re-invent the wheel. Another advantage is that it is available for free and is an open source software. Django is pretty fast, as it was designed to aid the developers in taking their applications from concept to launch in a short period of time.

Django installation

Before using Django, you have to get it installed. Following are the instructions for installing Django. First, you need to install Python, as it is a Python web framework. You can install Python 3 version for using Django. A lightweight database called SQLite is included with Python so that you will not need to get a database just yet. Get the latest version of Python from the internet or the package manager of your operating system. You may verify whether Python is installed by typing python from the shell. You will see things like these:

Python 3.x.y

[GCC 4.x] on linux

Type "help", "copyright", "credits" or "license" for more information.

>>>

Setting up a database is necessary only if you are going to work with large database engines such as MySQL, Oracle, or PostgreSQL. For installing these kinds of databases, consult the online database installation information. The actual Django installation is easy and can be done in 3 ways.

1. Installing an official version of Django, which is the best way for most users.

2. Installing a Django version supplied by the operating system distribution.

3. Installing the latest development version. The last option is aimed at enthusiasts who are looking for the greatest and latest features and are not afraid of running newer codes. It is quite possible that you will face new bugs in the development version, however, reporting them will help the Django development. Another factor is that it is less likely that the third party releases are compatible with the development version compared to the stable latest version.

Verification

To verify that Django will be noticed by Python, type python with the shell. When you reach the Python prompt, try to import Django:

>>> import django

>>> print(django.get_version())

2.2

This means that you have a Django version installed.

1. Installing the official release by using pip: As noted earlier, this is the recommended way of installing Django. First, install pip. The simplest way of doing this is by using the standalone pip installer. If your distribution has pip installed already, you might be required to update it in case it is outdated. You will know if it is outdated, as the installation will not work in that case.

Have a look at virtualenvwrapper and virtualenv, as the tools will provide an isolated environment for Python, and it is more practical than having system-wide installed packages. It is also allowed to use installing packages that do not allow administrator privileges. You can find online tutorials for creating virtual env. Once you have created and activated the virtual environment you need to enter this command:

$ pip install Django

2. Installing a package which is distribution specific: You can verify online whether your distribution or platform can provide official installers and packages. The packages with distribution provided typically allow automatic installation of the dependencies with simple upgrade routes, but these packages mostly do not contain the latest releases of Django.

3. Development version installation: If you have decided to utilize the latest development versions of Django, it will be a good idea to pay close attention to the provided development timeline. You may wish to keep an eye on the release notes provided for the upcoming releases. It will aid you in staying in touch with the new features that you might want to use and also the changes that will be required in the code while updating the new Django copy. For having stable releases, the necessary changes get documented on the release notes.

In case you want to be capable of updating the Django code

occasionally by having the latest fixes and improvements, go through these guidelines:

a. Ensure that you have git installed on your machine so that you will be able to run its commands with a shell. For testing this, enter git help at the shell prompt.

b. There is a main development branch of Django and you can get it like this:

$ git clone https://github.com/django/django.git

This creates a directory called Django in the current directory.

c. Ensure that your Python interpreter is capable of loading the Django code. The easiest way of doing this is by using virtualenvwrapper, virtualenv, and pip. You can find the tutorial online for creating the virtualenv.

d. Once you have set up and activated the virtualenv, you can run this command:

$ pip install -e django/

It will make the Django code importable and also will make available the Django-admin utility command. It means you are all set, in other words. If you need to update the Django source code copy you can run it through the command git pull from the Django directory. Once you do this, any changes will be automatically downloaded.

Reasons for using Django

By using Django, the web applications can be taken from concept to launch within a matter of a few hours. It takes out all the hassle associated with web development. Django arrived on the scene when the first wave of Rails hype was going up. Django was immediately dubbed as Python's answer to Rails, and that raised a few eyebrows immediately. These days, one of the most distinct advantages of learning Python is its capability to allow the use of Django. Django might be your answer to building your own app. It is gaining popularity due to its practical design and simplicity of use.

It is a web framework from the high-level Python and is basically a toolkit for web applications containing all the required components. The idea here is to allow the developers to concentrate on the new portions of their applications unique to the project rather than implementing the same codes over again. Django has many more features than some of the other frameworks out there. Django framework empowers you to model your domain and code classes, and you will do it fast.

1. Time-tested framework: You will often find that Django is one of the first frameworks that will respond to vulnerabilities. The core team normally alerts the other compatriots about the patches they need to make. There are many good things said about the Django stability and although all the bugs are not fixed, many have been. Nowadays, most Django releases focus on edge case concerns and newer features.

2. Accessibility to Django packages: There is a Django community much like the Python community, and it contributes lots of great packages and utilities for the developers. You can type Django in PyPi and you can find more than 4000 packages ready for use. This is the batteries included policy used by Django. This framework houses just about everything you might wish for.

3. Django is crowd-tested: Both Python and Django are a lot quieter compared to Rails and Node. They receive a lot of publicity from their major users. This doesn't mean that other major names do not use Django. You will find Django powering several of the internet's most popular and widely used sites, such as Pinterest and Instagram. Even Facebook uses Django for behind the scenes utilities. Django was designed to cater to the publishers, so it should come as no surprise to people that websites such as Smithsonian Magazine and The Washington Post make use of Django.

4. Django comes with useful documentation: Django arrived on the scene with documentation which was far better than any other open source project. It has only improved over a period of time. When it came out initially, the quality of documentation was one of the reasons why Django was in a class apart. Most other available frameworks at the time just used an alphabetical list containing modules, attributes and all methods. It works out quite well for references, but is not useful when you are starting new with the framework. The documentation quality of Django is not unique anymore, however, it remains one of the better examples of documentation for an open source software. Maintaining the quality of these documents is a constant concern for the developers of Django. Documents form a very significant part of the Django world.

5. The supportive Django community: It is often mentioned that the Python community is one of its better aspects. This is true for Django as well. Django Software

Foundation is the governing body of Django, and all the events involving Django come with a code of conduct. As a matter of fact, DSF has published statements taking an official stand on diversity and the Django community they envision. In several communities out there, things such as mailing lists and IRC are not welcome and are toxic many times. In this case, they are pleasant, although you are bound to find a rotten apple - but they get handled very fast. Thanks to the policies of the governing body, lots of groups such as Django Girls have flourished.

6. Django is a great advocator of SEO practices: It is a well-known fact that SEOs and web developers do not go well together. The work put in by the developers and optimization for the search engines always seem like cross purposes. This is less of an issue in the case of Django. The Django framework by Python advocates the use of humanly readable URLs of websites that help with the search engines, and they are not only useful from the user's perspective, but also for the use of keywords in the URLs while ranking the sites. The SEO team in such a case is bound to be grateful. It also makes sense to use URLs that are not a series of random numbers and alphabets, but actually mean something.

7. Scalable: Of course Django is great for those who are getting started, and surprisingly it is also good when we come down to scaling. At its heart, Django is a series of various components which are ready to go by default. As these components are decoupled, meaning they are not dependent on one another, they may be unplugged and replaced when the startup is in need of more specific solutions.

8. Security: By default, Django will prevent a whole range of usual security mistakes, which is better than, say, PHP. Django will camouflage or hide the website source code by dynamically creating web pages and sending the info through the templates to the web browsers. You cannot directly view the source code on the internet.

Summary

There is something about the way in which Django has been marketed, or the lack of any serious marketing for a long period of time. It is definitely a far cry from the way Rails was marketed. Until recently, the marketing efforts mostly consisted of people blogging or talking at PyCon, and then moving on to work on the framework. You could build amazing products by using Django and allowing the results to market for themselves. Nowadays, you will find the DjangoCon, DSF, and business-minded consultants conducting training sessions, and several books are available along with everything else. However, all this is pretty recent, and the other factors described above were more instrumental behind the steady rise in Django popularity since it was released.

Chapter 8: Python OOP

In this chapter, we will take a look at Object Oriented Programming, or OOP, in Python. We will see the basic concept with some examples. As we have explored earlier, Python is a multi-pattern programming language, so it supports various programming approaches. One of the popular methods for resolving the programming problems is through the creation of objects. It is known as OOP, or Object Oriented Programming. There are 2 basic characteristics of an object, which are behavior and attributes. Let's consider an example: If a parrot is an object, its age, name, and color are its attributes, and its singing and dancing are part of the behavior.

The OOP concept in Python focuses on the creation of reusable code. It is also known as a DRY (Don't Repeat Yourself) concept. The concept of OOP in Python has some basic principles like inheritance, encapsulation, and polymorphism. Inheritance is a process in which we use details of a new class without modifying the current class. Encapsulation means hiding the private details of the class from other objects, and polymorphism is using common operations in various ways for various data inputs.

Class

A class is a blueprint used for an object. We may imagine a class to be the sketch of a parrot having labels. It will contain all the requisite details of the parrot - name, size, color, etc. We can study the parrot based on this description. In this case, the parrot is the object. Here is an example of a class for a parrot:

```
class Parrot:

  pass
```

The class keyword is used here for defining an empty class Parrot. From this "Class" we can construct instances. An instance is a specific object developed from a specific class.

Object

An instantiation of the class is known as an object or an instance. When classes are defined, just the object description gets defined. There is no storage memory allocated. An example of an object of the parrot class is:

obj = Parrot()

In this case, obj is the object of the class Parrot. Let's suppose that we have all the parrot details. Now, we will see how to build a class and objects of parrot.

Example 1: Creating a class and an object in Python:

class Parrot:

class attribute

species = "bird"

instance attribute

def __init__(self, name, age):

self.name = name

```
self.age = age

# instantiate the Parrot class

blu = Parrot("Blu", 10)

woo = Parrot("Woo", 15)

# access the class attributes

print("Blu is a {}".format(blu.__class__.species))

print("Woo is also a {}".format(woo.__class__.species))

# access the instance attributes

print("{} is {} years old".format( blu.name, blu.age))

print("{} is {} years old".format( woo.name, woo.age))[44]
```

Once we run this program its output will be like this,

Blu is a bird

Woo is also a bird

Blu is 10 years old

Woo is 15 years old[45]

In the program above, we have created a class having name Parrot. After that, we have defined attributes which are the

[44] Parewa Labs Pvt. Ltd. https://www.programiz.com/python-programming/object-oriented-programming

[45] Parewa Labs Pvt. Ltd. https://www.programiz.com/python-programming/object-oriented-programming

characteristics of the object. Then we created instances of the class Parrot. Here "blu" and woo are the references to the new objects. After this, we have accessed the class attribute by using _class_.species. The class attributes are one and the same for all class instances. We can also access the instance attributes by using blu.name along with blu.age. But the instance attributes happen to be different for all instances of the classes.

Methods

Methods are the functions that are defined inside a class body. Methods are utilized for defining object behavior. Let's see an example depicting the creation of methods in Python:

class Parrot:

instance attributes

    def __init__(self, name, age):

    self.name = name

    self.age = age

instance method

def sing(self, song):

    return "{} sings {}".format(self.name, song)

def dance(self):

        return "{} is now dancing".format(self.name)

```
# instantiate the object
blu = Parrot("Blu", 10)


# call our instance methods
print(blu.sing("'Happy'"))
   print(blu.dance())
```

If we run this program, its output will be like this,

Blu sings 'Happy'

Blu is now dancing

In the program above, we have defined 2 methods and they are sing() and dance(). They are called instance methods, as they get called on the instance object blue.

Inheritance

Inheritance is the way by which you create a new class by using the details of existing classes without modifying them. The new class formed is a child class or a derived class. In the same manner, the existing class will be the base class or parent class. Now, let's see an example of inheritance in Python.

```
# parent class
class Bird:
```

```python
    def __init__(self):
        print("Bird is ready")
    def whoisThis(self):
        print("Bird")
    def swim(self):
        print("Swim faster")
# child class
class Penguin(Bird):
    def __init__(self):
# call super() function
        super().__init__()
        print("Penguin is ready")
    def whoisThis(self):
        print("Penguin")
    def run(self):
        print("Run faster")
peggy = Penguin()
peggy.whoisThis()
peggy.swim()
```

peggy.run() [46]

If we run the program above, we will get an output like this,

Bird is ready

Penguin is ready

Penguin

Swim faster

Run faster[47]

In the program above, we have created 2 classes viz. Bird (parent class) and Penguin (child class). The child class will inherit the functions of your parent class. This can be seen from the swim() method. The child class here modifies the parent class behavior. This can be seen from the WhoisThis () method. In addition to this, we can extend the functions of your parent class with creation of new run() method. We can also use super() function before the _int_() method. This is done because we wish to pull out the content of your _init_() method from your parent class inside the child class.

---

[46] Parewa Labs Pvt. Ltd. https://www.programiz.com/python-programming/object-oriented-programming
[47] Parewa Labs Pvt. Ltd. https://www.programiz.com/python-programming/object-oriented-programming

Encapsulation

By using the OOP in Python, we may restrict access to variables and methods. It prevents the data from undergoing direct modification, and it is called encapsulation. The private attributes in Python are denoted by using the prefix underscore. That is a single "_" or a double "__".

class Computer:

   def __init__(self):

     self.__maxprice = 900

   def sell(self):

     print("Selling Price: {}".format(self.__maxprice))

   def setMaxPrice(self, price):

     self.__maxprice = price

c = Computer()

c.sell()

change the price

c.__maxprice = 1000

c.sell()

using setter function

c.setMaxPrice(1000)

c.sell()[48]

Once we run the program above, its output will look like this:

Selling Price: 900

Selling Price: 900

Selling Price: 1000[49]

In this program above, we will define a class called Computer. We make use of __init__() method for storing the highest selling price of the computer. We have also tried to modify the price. But we cannot change it, as Python will treat the __maxprice as a private attribute. For changing this value, we have used a setter function that is setMaxPrice() which will take the price as a parameter.

---

[48] Parewa Labs Pvt. Ltd. https://www.programiz.com/python-programming/object-oriented-programming
[49] Parewa Labs Pvt. Ltd. https://www.programiz.com/python-programming/object-oriented-programming

Polymorphism

Polymorphism is the capability in OOP of using a common interface for several data types or forms. Suppose we are required to color a shape - you can find many shape options such as circle, square, or rectangle. But, we can use the same method for coloring any shape, and this is called polymorphism. Let's see an example of polymorphism in Python:

```python
class Parrot:

    def fly(self):
        print("Parrot can fly")


    def swim(self):
        print("Parrot can't swim")


class Penguin:

    def fly(self):
        print("Penguin can't fly")
```

```python
    def swim(self):
        print("Penguin can swim")


# common interface
def flying_test(bird):
    bird.fly()


#instantiate objects
blu = Parrot()
peggy = Penguin()


# passing the object
flying_test(blu)
flying_test(peggy)
```

Once you run the program above its output will be:

Parrot can fly

Penguin can't fly

In this program above, we have defined 2 classes: Parrot and Penguin. Each of the classes has a common method fly(). But the functions contained within them are different. For allowing polymorphism, we have created a common interface which is the flying_test() function and it may take all objects. After this we have passed the 2 objects blu and peggy in the function flying_test() which ran them effectively.

Chapter 9: Why Python for Machine Learning and Artificial Intelligence?

As we have learned, Python has slowly risen to the top in terms of popularity over the years and is now one of the leading programming languages in the world. You can find Python supporting applications ranging from scripting and web development to process automation. Python is one of the top choices among the developers for use in the fields of machine learning, artificial intelligence, and deep learning.

The advancement of artificial intelligence has created a range of new opportunities for applications developers. AI permits Spotify to recommend songs and artists, or allows Netflix to know what to show to you next. AI is also widely used by organizations working in customer service for driving self-service, improving the productivity of employees, and for improving workflow.

Now let's get to the relevant question. What is it that makes Python so useful for artificial intelligence? In this chapter, we will take a look at the significant reasons why this programming language is the go-to one for the machine learning and AI developers, and why you need to think about this choice for your next project related to AI.

Difference between AI, ML, and DL: However, before beginning, it may be useful to understand the difference between ML, AI, and Deep Learning. In a straightforward language, deep learning is machine learning subset and artificial intelligence is a general category which holds machine learning. AI refers to all the intelligence displayed by a machine and which leads to a suboptimal or optimal solution to a problem. ML takes this concept a step further with the use of algorithms for parsing the data and learning from it to make informed decisions.

Deep learning is similar to this, but has a different set of capabilities such as the capability to draw conclusions in a way that is reminiscent of human decision making. Deep learning does this with the use of a layered structure of algorithms which are a takeoff on the neural network working inside a human brain. As a result, a model is created which is capable of learning multiple levels of representation and corresponds to various abstraction levels.

Python as a choice for AI: Python is the favored programming language for developers working in a range of different applications. However, what makes Python particularly good for AI projects? Let's take a look at the reasons.

1. Great collection of frameworks and libraries: One of the most important reasons for Python being such a popular choice generally is its abundance of frameworks and libraries facilitating the coding and saving the development time period. Python caters to machine learning and deep learning exceptionally well. NumPv can be used for science-related computations, SciPv advanced scientific computation, and scikit-learn is used for data analysis and data mining. These are among the most used libraries, and they work with some heavy frameworks such as TensorFlow, Apache Spark, and CNTK. In terms of deep learning and machine learning, these frameworks and libraries are Python-first kind, and in fact some of them such as PyTorch are written for Python specifically.

2. Simplicity: Python is famous for the readable and concise code, and it is unparalleled when you talk about simplicity and ease of use, especially for new developers. It has several advantages that can be used for deep learning and machine learning. Both DL and ML rely on complex algorithms along with multi-stage workflows. Therefore, the less developers have to worry about the intricacies of the code, the more they can focus on finding solutions to the problems and achieving the project targets.

The simple syntax used by Python means that it is a lot faster during development than other programming languages, and it allows the developers to test the algorithms quickly without having to actually implement them. In addition to this, the readable code is indispensable for collaborative coding. It is a great asset to have when the same project in deep learning or machine learning changes hands within different development teams. This is especially true when a project contains a good deal of customized business logic or 3rd party components.

3. Great support: By now, we know that Python is an open source language and is supported via many resources and high-quality documentation. It also has a big and active developer community, which is helpful in providing advice and assistance at all stages of the development procedure.

4. Flexibility and platform independence: Python is independent of platforms and as a result, it is one of the most popular and flexible choices for AI use across various platforms and technologies. You can achieve the desired results with small tweaks in the basic code. Python also provides options for selecting between the OOP approach and scripting. You might use IDE as well to check out most of the codes, and this is a great help for the developers struggling with various algorithms.

5. Faster prototyping: Apart from the frameworks, the quick prototyping makes Python a significant programming language which cannot be ignored. Remember, AI requires plenty of research, and therefore it is necessary that they are not dependent on the 500 KB boilerplate code used in Java for testing a new hypothesis. This will never finish the project on time. Whereas in Python, almost all ideas maybe be quickly validated via 20-30 code lines (same as JS with libs). So, Python is extremely useful for AI purposes.

Python vs. C++ for artificial intelligence

When used for artificial intelligence, Python is more popular than C++ and it leads in the survey among developers with 57% votes. This is because it is easier to learn Python and implement it. With the several libraries it has, the programming language may also be utilized for data analysis. C++ will provide better performance than Python, and this is because C++ is a statically typed language, and so there is no likelihood of typing errors during the runtime. C++ also develops a quicker and more compact runtime code.

Python, on the other hand, is a dynamic programming language and will reduce complexity in case of collaboration. This means that you may implement functionality by using lesser code. Unlike C++, where all the important compilers have a tendency to perform specific optimization and tend to be specific to the platform, Python code will run on almost all platforms without wasting time on configurations.

Due to the advent of GPU-accelerated computing, we are offered parallel capabilities that lead to the creation of libraries like CUDA Python and cuDNN in Python, and this gives it an edge over C++. It means that more of the actual computing will be offloaded to the GPUs and as a result, any performance advantage held by C++ becomes rousingly irrelevant. Python will also outdo C++ in terms of simplicity of code, as it is vitally important for new developers. C++ is a lower-level language and needs greater skills and experience to master.

The simple syntax used by Python allows for more intuitive and natural ETL (Extract, Transform, Load) procedures. This will also lead to faster development compared to C++, allowing the developers to test ML algorithms without the need to implement them faster. So overall, Python has an edge over C++ and is more suitable for AI.

Python vs. Java for artificial intelligence

Even while mastering the programming of artificial intelligence in Java, it is necessary to know where Java stands in comparison with Python. Remember, Python is an interpreted language, while Java is a compiled programming language. These 2 programming languages are written differently as well. Any structure of Java is enclosed in brackets, while Python makes use of indentation for performing similar tasks. Java is also slower in terms of performance than Python, and for the development of higher-end applications for AI Python is definitely preferred over Java. The artificial intelligence library of Java is its answer to Python, however, it is still less accessible than Python to the developers for obvious reasons. Java's modern Norvig Russell approach to AI has created a way for several developers to sit back and take note of the fact that it is the best language for neural networks.

Summary

Artificial intelligence has a profound effect on the world we are living in, and new applications are emerging all the time. The smarter developers are going for Python as the priority programming language due to the range of benefits it offers. Due to this, it is particularly suitable for deep learning and machine learning related projects.

The extensive libraries of Python that are specific to machine learning along with the available frameworks make the development process pretty simple and cut the time for development. The simple syntax and readability of Python advocates quick testing of complex algorithms and also makes the language more accessible to the non-programmers and new programmers. The cognitive overhead is also reduced for the developers and frees up your mental resources so that you may concentrate more on issue-resolution and achieving the target of the project.

Although other programming languages may also be used for AI related projects, there is no denying the fact that the cutting edge is provided by Python and must be given the due consideration while selecting the programming language.

Chapter 10: Examples of Python Programming Language Interview Questions and Answers

Python has reached the number 3 position on the list of the most sought after programming languages in the world. Here are some of essential interview questions for Python to get you acquainted with the knowledge and skills necessary for succeeding in job interviews. You will find a good balance between practical questions and theory questions here to achieve the full advantage. Apart from the aspirants for jobs, even the recruiters might want to refer to this chapter for a set of proper questions to evaluate a candidate.

1. ***What is Python and what are its benefits? What is the meaning of PEP 8?***

Answer: Python happens to be one of the most popular and a successful interpreted programming languages in the world. If you write a script in Python, it is not necessary to compile it before execution. Some other interpreted languages available are JavaScript and PHP.

Benefits: It is a dynamically typed language, meaning that there is no need to mention the data type of your variables at the time of declaration. Python allows the setting of variables such as var1=101 and var2="You are an engineer." without showing any errors. Python will support OOP, as you may define classes with inheritance and composition. Python doesn't need access specifiers such as private or public.

The Python functions are like first class objects. It will suggest that you should assign them to your variables, return them from other methods and also pass them as arguments.

Development by using Python is pretty fast but running the code is often slower than the compiled languages. However, Python empowers you with C language extensions, and so you may optimize the scripts. Python has many applications like in web development, data modeling, test automation, big data analytics and so on. You may also use Python as the glue layer for working with other programming languages.

PEP 8: The latest coding standard used in Python is called PEP 8, and it is a set of coding recommendations. It will guide and deliver a readable Python code.

2. What will be the output of this fragment of Python code? Justify the answer.

```
def extendList(val, list=[]):

    list.append(val)

    return list


list1 = extendList(10)

list2 = extendList(123,[])

list3 = extendList('a')


print "list1 = %s" % list1

print "list2 = %s" % list2

print "list3 = %s" % list3
```[50]

---

[50] Harsh S. 100 Essential Python Interview Questions (Edition 2019).

Answer: This code snippet from Python will print the result as:

list1 = [10, 'a']

list2 = [123]

list3 = [10, 'a']

You might incorrectly expect the list1 to equate to, [10] and expect the list3 matching with ['a']. And the justification being that the list argument gets initialized to the default value every time you place a call to extendList. The flow here is that a new list will be created when the function is defined and will be used when someone calls the method extendList without list arguments. It works in this manner because calculation of expressions within default arguments will occur at the time when function is defined and not during the invocation.

The 2 lists List1 and List3 are thus operating on exactly the same list. But the list2 will run on another object created on its own with passing of an empty list as the list parameter value. The extendList function definition gets modified in this manner:

def extendList(val, list=None):

  if list is None:

    list = []

  list.append(val)

  return list[51]

(2019). https://www.techbeamers.com/python-interview-questions-programmers/

[51] Harsh S. 100 Essential Python Interview Questions (Edition 2019).

By using the revised implementation your output will be:

list1 = [10]

list2 = [123]

list3 = ['a']

3. What statement will you use in Python in case it does not require any action but requires proper syntax?

Answer: Null operation can be done by using the pass statement. Nothing will happen when it is executed. The pass keyword is to be used in lowercase. In case you write Pass you will get an error such as "NameError: name Pass is not defined." Remember that the Python statements happen to be case sensitive.

letter = "hai sethuraman"

for i in a letter:

  if i == "a":

    pass

    print("pass statement is executed..............")

  else:

    print(i)

(2019). https://www.techbeamers.com/python-interview-questions-programmers/

4. State the procedure to get the Home directory by using ~ in Python.

Answer: You will be required to import the "os" module and then a single line will do the remaining.

import os

print (os.path.expanduser('~'))

Output:

/home/runner

5. Which are the different Python built-in types?

Answer: These are the most commonly used Python built-in types:

Python immutable built-in data types: These include strings, numbers, and tuples.

Python mutable built-in data types: These include dictionaries, lists, and sets.

6. How do you find issues or perform the static analysis in any Python application?

Answer: You may use PyChecker, which happens to be the static analyzer. It will identify bugs in your Python project and reveal the complexity and style related bugs. There is another tool called Pylint which will check whether the coding standards of the Python module are satisfied.

7. What is the use of Python decorator?

Answer: A relative change you do to the Python syntax for adjusting the functions quickly is called Python decorator.

8. What is the main difference between a list and a tuple?

Answer: The major difference between a tuple and a list is that the latter is mutable and the tuple is not. You may hash the tuple, for example, while using it in the dictionaries as a key.

9. How is memory management handled in Python?

Answer: Private heaps are used by Python to maintain memory. Therefore, the heaps hold all Python objects and data structures. The area is accessible only to Python interpreter and programmers cannot use it. The private heap is handled by the memory manager of Python. The memory manager allocates the memory for the Python objects. There is a built-in garbage collector employed by Python which will salvage all the unused memory and will offload it into the heap space.

10. What are the main differences between a def and a lambda?

Lambda vs. Def

Def is capable of holding multiple expressions, and lambda is a single expression function. Def will generate a function and will designate a name to it for calling it later, while lambda creates a function and returns it. Def may have a return statement while lambda cannot. It is possible to use lambda inside a dictionary and a list.

11. Can you write a Reg Expression which confirms one email ID by using the "Re" a Python Reg Expression Module?

Python comes with a regular expression module called "re." Check out the expression "re" which will check the email ID for .co.in and .com subdomains.

import re

```
print(re.search(r"[0-9a-zA-Z.]+@[a-zA-
Z]+\.(com|co\.in)$","micheal.pages@mp.com"))
```

12. What will be the output of this code fragment? Can you find any error in the written code?

list = ['a', 'b', 'c', 'd', 'e']

print (list[10:])

The output of the lines of code written above is []. It will not give any error such as IndexError. You need to know that trying to get a member of a list by using the index which exceeds member count, for example, an attempt to access list[10] as provided in the query, will give an IndexError. But remember that retrieving just a slice at your starting index which surpasses the number of items in your list will not result in IndexError. This will only return an empty list.

13. Do you have a case or a switch statement in Python? If not, what's the reason for this?

Answer: No. Python does not contain a switch statement, however, you may write a switch function and use it.

14. What built-in function does Python use for iterating over the number sequence?

Range() will generate a list of numbers that is utilized for iterating over for the loops.

for i in range(5):

   print(i)

There are 2 sets of parameters accompanying the range()

function. First is range(stop). Stop is the number of integers to be generated and it will start from zero. For example, range(3) == [0, 1, 2]. The 2nd is range([start], stop[, step]). Start is the starting number for the sequence. Stop will specify the upper limit for the sequence, and Step is the increment factor for generation of the sequence.

Notes: It is important to note here that just the integer arguments are permitted. Parameters may be positive or negative. The Python range() function will start from zero index.

15. What optional statements of Python are possible inside the Try-Except block?

Answer: You may use 2 optional clauses inside the try-except block, the first of which is the "else" clause. This is necessary when you wish to run a code piece while the try block is not creating an exception. Second is the "finally" clause, which is useful when you wish to execute steps that run irrespective of whether there is an exception or not.

16. What are strings in Python?

Answer: The strings in Python are a sequence of alpha-numeric characters. They are immutable objects, meaning that it is not possible to alter them once they have been assigned a value. Python will provide many methods like the join(), split(), or replace() for altering the strings. However, none of these will change the original object.

17. What is the slicing operation in Python?

Answer: It is a string operation to extract a string part or some list part. In Python, the strings start at index 0 and then the nth character will store at the text[n-1] position. Reverse index is also possible in Python that is in a backward direction with help from negative numbers. The slice in Python also happens to be a constructor function that generates slice objects. Its result is a set of indices that are noted with range(step, stop, start). The slicing method will allow three parameters. First is the start, which specifies the starting number for the slicing to start. Second is the stop. It is the number that indicates the end of slicing. And the third is the step, which is a value that increments after every index and the default value is 1.

18. What is the meaning of %S in Python?

Answer: Python provides support for the formatting of all values in a string. It might consist of pretty complex expressions. One of the most common uses is pushing values in a string with the help of %s format specifiers. This formatting operation for Python has similar syntax to the C function printf().

19. Are strings mutable or immutable in Python?

Answer: The Python strings are definitely immutable. Let us consider an example. We have one "str" variable that holds a string value. It is not possible to mutate the container that is the string. But we may modify the contents of the string, which means the variable value.

20. What is an index in Python?

Answer: The index is an integer kind of data type that denotes a position within the ordered lists or strings. In Python, the strings are also the lists of various characters. We may access the strings by using the index that begins from 0 and moves to minus one. For instance, in this string "Program" indexing will happen this way:

Program 0 1 2 3 4 5

21. What are docstrings in Python?

Answer: The docstring is a unique text which is the first statement of these Python constructs, function, module, class, or method definition. The docstring will be added to the __doc__attribute of your string object. You can read some online queries regarding functions in Python in the interview questions.

22. What is a function in Python?

Answer: The function is a reusable entity and it is an object that represents a code block. It will bring modularity to your program and a high degree of reusability of code. There are many built-in functions provided by Python like print(), and they provide the capability to develop user-defined functions.

23. How many fundamental kinds of functions do you get in Python?

Answer: There are two fundamental kinds of functions in Python. The first is built-in and the second is user-defined. The built-in functions are a part of Python programming language, and some of them include print(), dir(), abs(), and len() etc.

24. How do you write a function in Python?

Answer: We may develop a Python function in this manner.

- Step 1: For starting the function, begin writing with the keyword def and then write the name of the function.
- Step 2: Now, it is possible to pass arguments and enclose them by using parentheses. The colon at the end marks the function header end.
- Step 3: After hitting Enter, we may add the required statements of Python for the execution.

25. What is a callable object or a function call in Python?

Answer: The function of Python is treated as a callable object. The function may allow some arguments and might also return a value or several values in a tuple form. There are other constructs available apart from functions, like classes or class instances that fit in the same category.

26. What's the return keyword used for?

Answer: The function is responsible for receiving the input and returning some output. The return happens to be a Python statement that can be used in a function to send a value back to the caller.

27. What do you mean by "call by value" in Python?

Answer: In the case of "call by value," the argument which could be a value or an expression will get bound to the corresponding variable of the function. Python will treat this variable as local in the scope of the function. If you make any changes to the variable it will remain local, and it does not reflect on the outside of the function.

28. What do you mean by the call by reference in Python?

Answer: It is possible to use both "pass by reference" and "call by reference" interchangeably. Once we pass an argument by reference, then it becomes available for the implicit reference to a function instead of being a simple copy. In this case, any readjustment to this argument will be visible to the function caller. It also allows more time and better space efficiency, as it takes you away from the requirement of creating local copies.

On the other hand, the disadvantage is that a variable may get changed accidentally during the calling of function, therefore, the programmers must handle the code carefully to avoid such uncertainties.

29. What is the role of the "Continue" in Python?

Answer: Continue is a jump statement for Python that moves the execution control of the next iteration in the loop and it leaves all other instructions of the block unexecuted. This Continue statement can be used in cases of both "for" and "while" loops.

30. Does Python come with a Main() method?

Answer: Main() is an entry point function which gets called initially in all the programming languages. As Python happens to be interpreter based, it will sequentially execute the line of code one-by-one. The programming language does come with the Main method. However, it will be executed when Python scripts run either on clicking it directly or when it starts from the command line. We may also override the default main() function in Python by utilizing the if statement. See the code below:

```
print("Welcome")

print("__name__ contains: ", __name__)

def main():

    print("Testing the main function")

if __name__ == '__main__':

    main()
```

Its output is,

Welcome

__name__ contains: __main__

Testing the main function[52]

31. What's the use of End in Python?

Answer: The print() function of Python will always print a new line at the end. The print() function will accept optional parameters known as End. The value of end by default is '\n'. The end character may be changed in the print statement with a value of our choice while making use of the parameter.

Example: Print a instead of the new line in the end.

print("Let's learn" , end = ' ')

print("Python")

Printing a dot in the end.

print("Learn to code from techbeamers" , end = '.')

print("com", end = ' ')

Its output is,

Let's learn Python

Learn to code from techbeamers.com[53]

---

[52] Harsh S. 100 Essential Python Interview Questions (Edition 2019). (2019). https://www.techbeamers.com/python-interview-questions-programmers/

[53] Harsh S. 100 Essential Python Interview Questions (Edition 2019). (2019). https://www.techbeamers.com/python-interview-questions-

32.   What is the use of a Break in Python?

Answer: Break statement is provided by Python for exiting from a loop. If a break appears in a code, the program control immediately exits from the loop body. Break statement inside a nested loop will cause the control to exit from the iterative inner block.

33.   What are whitespaces in Python?

Answer: Whitespaces represent characters that are used for separation and spacing. An empty representation is envisaged here, and it may be a space or a tab.

34.   What is the use of the Title() method in Python?

Answer: Python gives you the title() method for converting the first letter in every word for the capital format as the rest turns to a lowercase.

#Example

str = 'lEaRn pYtHoN'

print(str.title())

Its output is:

Learn Python

35.   What is the difference between Python and CPython?

Answer: The core of CPython is developed in C. Its prefix C will represent the fact and it runs the interpreter loop utilized for translating the Python-like code into C language.

---

programmers/

36. Which package will you buy to have the fastest form of Python?

Answer: PyPy will provide maximum capabilities while using CPython implementation to improve the performance. Different tests confirm that PyPy is about 5 times quicker than CPython. At the moment it supports Python 2.7.

37. How are the Python threads made safe?

Answer: Python will ensure safe access to the threads. It makes use of GIL mutex for setting synchronization. If a thread loses GIL lock at any point in time, then you must ensure that the code thread is safe. For instance, several of the Python operations execute in atomic fashion like calling of sort() method from a list.

38. How is the memory managed by Python?

Answer: Python will implement a heap manager internally that will hold all the objects of Python along with data structures. This heap manager does the memory allocation and de-allocation for the objects.

39. What are the set objects in Python?

Answer: Sets are nothing but an unordered collection of different objects in Python. These sets store immutable and unique objects. The implementation of Python is derived out of mathematics.

40. Are the Python lists the same as linked lists?

Answer: The Python lists are variable length arrays that are different from the C-style linked lists. Internally the list has a contiguous array for referencing other objects and will store a pointer to the array variable along with its length in the structure of the list head.

41. What are the classes in Python?

Answer: Python supports OOP (Object Oriented Programming) and provides almost all features of OOP for use in programs. The Python class is a blueprint for the creation of objects. It will define member variables and get the behavior associated with them. You may create them by using the keyword class. An object will be created from the constructor. The object will represent an instance of your class. In Python, we will generate instances and classes in this manner:

>>>class Human: # Create the class

...   pass

>>>man = Human() # Create the instance

>>>print(man)

<__main__.Human object at 0x0000000003559E10> [54]

42.   What are the attributes and methods of a class?

Answer: A class is of no use if it doesn't have any functionality defined. This can be done by the addition of attributes. They will work as containers for functions and data. The attribute can be added directly by specification inside the class body:

>>> class Human:

...   profession = "programmer" # specify the attribute 'profession' of the class

>>> man = Human()

_____

[54] Harsh S. 100 Essential Python Interview Questions (Edition 2019). (2019). https://www.techbeamers.com/python-interview-questions-programmers/

>>> print(man.profession)

programmer[55]

After the addition of attributes, we will go on and define our functions. Normally they are called methods. In your method signature, it is always necessary to provide first arguments with self-keywords:

>>> class Human:

   profession = "programmer"

   def set_profession(self, new_profession):

     self.profession = new_profession

>>> man = Human()

>>> man.set_profession("Manager")

>>> print(man.profession)

Manager[56]

43. How do you assign values to the classes attributes during runtime?

Answer: It is possible to specify values at runtime for the

---

[55] Harsh S. 100 Essential Python Interview Questions (Edition 2019). (2019). https://www.techbeamers.com/python-interview-questions-programmers/

[56] Harsh S. 100 Essential Python Interview Questions (Edition 2019). (2019). https://www.techbeamers.com/python-interview-questions-programmers/

attributes. Here it is necessary to add the init method and pass the input to the object constructor. See the following example of demonstrating this:

>>> class Human:

    def __init__(self, profession):

        self.profession = profession

    def set_profession(self, new_profession):

        self.profession = new_profession

>>> man = Human("Manager")

>>> print(man.profession)

Manager[57]

44. *What is a composition in Python?*

Answer: Composition is also a kind of inheritance in Python. Composition tends to inherit out of the base class, albeit a little differently than with the use of the instance variable of your base class acting as the derived class member. See the diagram below for clarification:

---

[57] Harsh S. 100 Essential Python Interview Questions (Edition 2019). (2019). https://www.techbeamers.com/python-interview-questions-programmers/

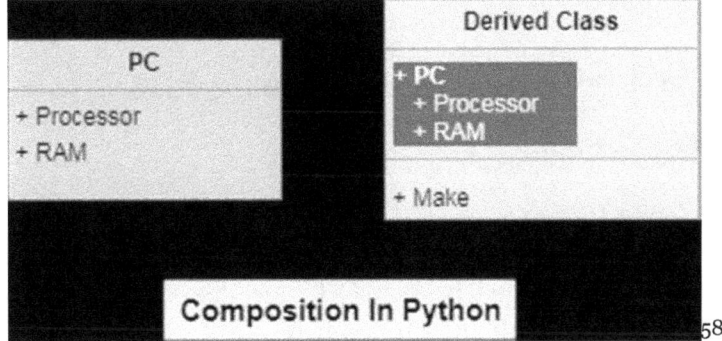

Composition In Python

For demonstrating the composition, it is essential to instantiate other objects in your class and then use the instances.

class PC: # Base class

　processor = "Xeon" # Common attribute

　def __init__(self, processor, ram):

　　self.processor = processor

　　self.ram = ram

　def set_processor(self, new_processor):

　　processor = new_processor

　def get_PC(self):

　　return "%s cpu & %s ram" % (self.processor, self.ram)

class Tablet():

　make = "Intel"

_____

58 Harsh S. 100 Essential Python Interview Questions (Edition 2019). (2019). https://www.techbeamers.com/python-interview-questions-programmers/

```
def __init__(self, processor, ram, make):

    self.PC = PC(processor, ram) # Composition

    self.make = make

def get_Tablet(self):

    return "Tablet with %s CPU & %s ram by %s" %
(self.PC.processor, self.PC.ram, self.make)

if __name__ == "__main__":

    tab = Tablet("i7", "16 GB", "Intel")

    print(tab.get_Tablet())
```

Its output is:

Tablet with i7 CPU & 16 GB ram by Intel

45.   What are exceptions and errors in Python?

Answer: The coding issues you encounter in a program are called errors. They might result in the program exiting abnormally. On the other hand, the exceptions happen due to the occurrence of external events which interrupt the usual flow of a program.

46.   What are Python closures?

Answer: The function objects returned by other functions are called as Python closures. They are used for eliminating the code redundancy. See the following example. Here we have a straightforward closure for multiplying the numbers:

```
def multiply_number(num):

    def product(number):

        'product() here is a closure'

        return num * number

    return product

num_2 = multiply_number(2)

print(num_2(11))

print(num_2(24))

num_6 = multiply_number(6)

print(num_6(1))[59]
```

Its output is:

22

48

6

47. How will you add elements to your dictionary in Python?

Answer: We may add elements to the dictionary by modification of the dictionary by using a fresh key and then set a value to it.

---

[59] Harsh S. 100 Essential Python Interview Questions (Edition 2019). (2019). https://www.techbeamers.com/python-interview-questions-programmers/

```
>>> # Setup a blank dictionary

>>> site_stats = {}

>>> site_stats['site'] = 'google.com'

>>> site_stats['traffic'] = 10000000000

>>> site_stats['type'] = 'Referral'

>>> print(site_stats)
```

{'type': 'Referral', 'site': 'google.com', 'traffic': 10000000000}
[60]

Now we will be able to join 2 dictionaries and get a larger dictionary by using the update() method.

```
>>> site_stats['site'] = 'google.co.in'

>>> print(site_stats)
```

{'site': 'google.co.in'}

```
>>> site_stats_new = {'traffic': 1000000, "type": "social media"}

>>> site_stats.update(site_stats_new)

>>> print(site_stats)
```

{'type': 'social media', 'site': 'google.co.in', 'traffic': 1000000} [61]

---

[60] Harsh S. 100 Essential Python Interview Questions (Edition 2019). (2019). https://www.techbeamers.com/python-interview-questions-programmers/
[61] Harsh S. 100 Essential Python Interview Questions (Edition 2019).

48. *What is the dictionary comprehension syntax in Python?*

Answer: The dictionary has a similar syntax as the list comprehension, albeit with the difference that it makes use of curly brackets.

{ aKey, itsValue for aKey in iterable }

For instance, the code below returns all the numbers from 10 to 20 in the form of keys, and it will store the squares of these numbers as values.

>>> adict = {var:var**2 for var in range(10, 20)}

>>> print(adict)

49. *How do you write conditional expressions in Python?*

Answer: We may use the following single statement as the conditional expression.

default_statement if Condition else another_statement.

>>> no_of_days = 366

>>> is_leap_year = "Yes" if no_of_days == 366 else "No"

>>> print(is_leap_year)

Yes[62]

(2019). https://www.techbeamers.com/python-interview-questions-programmers/
[62] Harsh S. 100 Essential Python Interview Questions (Edition 2019). (2019). https://www.techbeamers.com/python-interview-questions-programmers/

50.   *How do the ternary operators work in Python?*

Answer: The ternary operators are an alternative to your conditional statements. The operator combines a true or a false value to a statement which you will need to test. Its syntax looks like this:

[onTrue] if [Condition] else [onFalse]

x, y = 35, 75

smaller = x if x < y else y

print(smaller)

Conclusion

Python is an interpreted, OOP compliant, and high-level programming language with dynamic semantics. It has high-level and built-in data structures together with dynamic binding and typing. All of this makes it a very attractive proposition for quick application development and for using it as glue or scripting language for connecting the existing components together. It comes with an easy and simple to learn syntax, and it emphasizes the readability and also decreases the cost of maintaining your programs. Python supports different modules and packages which boost program modularity and code reuse. The extensive standard library which is offered with Python along with the interpreter is available in binary or source forms without any charges for the major platforms, and they may be freely distributed.

Programmers mostly love Python due to the better productivity it provides. As there are no compilation steps involved, the whole cycle of edit-test-debug is unbelievably fast. It is easy to debug the Python programs and any bugs or bad inputs never cause segmentation issues. Rather, when an error is discovered by the interpreter, it will raise an exception. If the program doesn't catch exceptions, the interpreter will print a stack trace. The source level debugger permits local and global variable inspection, arbitrary expression evaluation, stepping through the code lines, and setting breakpoints. The debugger is written in the same programming language which is a testimony to the introspective power of Python. Another quick way of debugging a program is by adding some print statements to the source. Python's speedy edit-test-debug cycle makes its straightforward approach extremely effective.

If you compare Python to R, you will find that Python is better at data manipulation and repetitive tasks, while R is better at exploring the data sets and ad hoc analysis. You will find R to have a steep learning curve, and those with no previous programming knowledge and experience will find it to be an overwhelming experience. Python is considered to be far simpler to learn. Hopefully this book has opened your eyes to the possibilities Python provides and has served as a guide to get you on your way to being a Python programming wiz.

Bibliography

Python – The new generation Language. Retrieved from https://www.geeksforgeeks.org/python-the-new-generation-language/

Krishelle Hardson-Hurley. 11 Beginner Tips for Learning Python Programming. (2018). https://realpython.com/python-beginner-tips/

A Quick Tour of Python Language Syntax. (2016). https://jakevdp.github.io/WhirlwindTourOfPython/02-basic-python-syntax.html

Jake VanderPlas. Basic Python Semantics: Variables and Objects. (2016). https://jakevdp.github.io/WhirlwindTourOfPython/03-semantics-variables.html

Jake VanderPlas. Basic Python Semantics: Control flow. (2016).

https://jakevdp.github.io/WhirlwindTourOfPython/07-control-flow-statements.html

HackerEarth. Expressions. (2019). https://www.hackerearth.com/practice/python/working-with-data/expressions/tutorial/

Jake VanderPlas. Built-In Types: Simple Values

. (2016). https://jakevdp.github.io/WhirlwindTourOfPython/05-built-in-scalar-types.html

Real Python. Python 3 Installation & Setup Guide. (2018). https://realpython.com/installing-python/

Data Structures.
https://python.swaroopch.com/data_structures.html

Parewa Labs Pvt. Ltd. https://www.programiz.com/python-programming/object-oriented-programming

Harsh S. 100 Essential Python Interview Questions (Edition 2019). (2019). https://www.techbeamers.com/python-interview-questions-programmers/

9 781952 340116